WHAT PEOPLE ARE SAYING ABOUT

TRANSCENDENT VOCATION

In the future, this book will be a primary resources for researchers, l now, it will have a much more imme and honest chronicle of the malevolen England's current stance over same-se  love and service which gay clergy continue to offer the Church despite everything.

The Revd Professor Diarmaid MacCulloch
Professor of the History of the Church, University of Oxford

Dr Maxwell's research analyses the systemic hypocrisy with which the Church of England treats its gay clergy and the widespread damage it has caused. By trying to appease a minority of extremists in the name of unity, it has scapegoated the honest, undermined its integrity and compromised its mission. The book's conclusion is an urgent call for leadership with the moral courage to tell the truth, and a new policy which respects the conscience of all.

The Very Revd Dr Jeffrey John
Dean of St Albans

This is a book that is long overdue. It will not make for comfortable reading for all who share the Christian faith. It has been written with a tender pen and as a result is a fascinating journey which takes us into the heart of those who are Gay and Christian.

The Revd Peter Owen Jones
Religious writer and broadcaster

Another helpful ingredient in the process of showing bishops and others who need to understand where gay clergy actually are in the Church that healthy ministry by gay clergy continues in spite of 'Issues' as policy.

The Revd Colin Coward
Director, Changing Attitude

Transcendent Vocation

Why Gay Clergy Tolerate Hypocrisy

Transcendent Vocation

Why Gay Clergy Tolerate Hypocrisy

Sarah Maxwell

CHRISTIAN
ALTERNATIVE

Winchester, UK
Washington, USA

First published by Christian Alternative Books, 2013
Christian Alternative Books is an imprint of John Hunt Publishing Ltd., Laurel House,
Station Approach, Alresford, Hants, SO24 9JH, UK
office1@jhpbooks.net
www.johnhuntpublishing.com
www.christian-alternative.com

For distributor details and how to order please visit the 'Ordering' section on our website.

Text copyright: Sarah Maxwell 2012

ISBN: 978 1 78099 918 0

A CIP catalogue record for this book is available from the British Library.

Design: Stuart Davies

Printed and bound by CPI Group (UK) Ltd, Croydon, CR0 4YY

We operate a distinctive and ethical publishing philosophy in all
areas of our business, from our global network of authors to
production and worldwide distribution.

CONTENTS

ACKNOWLEDGEMENTS   x

CHAPTER 1: INTRODUCTION   1

CHAPTER 2: SIGNIFICANT EVENTS AND
    PUBLICATIONS: 1967-2007   9

CHAPTER 3: FORTY YEARS OF TURNING POINTS   31
The 1967 decriminalisation of homosexuality, or
    "We didn't know anything about it"   33
What a difference an Act makes, or "It was easier
    before it became legal"   35
The Seventies – Liberality creeping in   37
The Eighties – The run-up to Higton   39
The Higton Debate – a turning point?   42
Negative feelings about 'Issues', or "Why not 'Issues
    in Aardvark Sexuality'?"   44
The 1998 Lambeth Conference – a turning point?   46
Jeffery John – a turning point?   47
The Noughties – Polarisation rules ok.   50

CHAPTER 4: THE OXYMORON OF GAY PRIESTS   57
The ironies of Issues' conclusion, or "The whole
    thing is messy"   57
Attitudes to lay authority for homosexuals, or "People
    of good conscience"   59
Priestly changes, or "A strange idea to start with" 61
Gay clergy: not allowed, but lots anyway   63
Gay clergy: not allowed, so how do they cope?   65
"Always at the mercy of bishops" – Episcopal attitudes 69

Partners and lodgers – "Is that "lodger" with a small l
    or a big L?" 72
Chances of preferment, or "It would be a hopeless case." 75
Congregational response or "People will cut you
    almost infinite slack." 76
Consideration for others, or "The sin is disturbing
    the harmony" 79
"Don't ask, don't tell" – a long standing approach 80

CHAPTER 5: THE PROBLEM OF CIVIL PARTNERSHIPS 86
Civil Partnership: The Church's official line and
    the reality 88
Same-sex blessings: The Church's official line and
    the reality 91
Civil Partnership: "He is my partner, not my husband,"
    or Not marriage 93

CHAPTER 6: DIVERGENCE FROM SOCIETY 97
A Different World, or "Constant liberalisation" 98
A Different World, or "Everything is possible but
    nothing is forgivable" 101
A Different Church, or "Not the same church as the
    one that I was ordained into" 104

CHAPTER 7: BIBLICAL INTERPRETATION 109
The Bible says homosexuality is wrong, or "A pretty
    sort of simple position" 110
Biblical condemnations, or "Singled out because it's sex" 111
Use of the Bible: "Picking and Choosing" 113
Use of the Bible: "A Gospel of Hatred?" 114
Divine inspiration: its changing nature 116

CHAPTER 8: SEXUAL IDENTITY 121

Genetically determined so morally neutral, or "Like
 having dark hair or eyes" 122

Changing views, or "Maturity and grace" 126

Popular stereotypical presuppositions, or "I'm not
 dressed in a pink leotard" 128

Our sexuality, or "What I believe is just me" 130

The importance of how homosexuality is exercised:
 "Permanent, faithful, stable" 133

CHAPTER 9: THE TRANSCENDENT VOCATION 137

Why they stay, or "Called by God" 137

Vocation as a homosexual, or "God calling me with
 my sexuality" 143

The Transcendent Vocation, or "For better or worse" 146

REFERENCES 152

ACKNOWLEDGEMENTS

This book would not exist without the support of a number of people. I should like to express my debt of gratitude to the following:

Friends and family who offered advice and encouragement to persevere both during my time as a research student and when I was subsequently exploring publication, especially my former colleague Ann Peters and my cousin Jenny Sinclair.

Those at the University of Chichester who guided and encouraged me during the research project, especially Gill Kester.

The clergymen who welcomed me into their homes and allowed me to interview them, especially the gay clergy who were gracious enough to entrust me with sensitive personal information. Not only do I want to thank them, but I want to assure them that there is nothing in this book that will disclose their identity. It is my hope that a day will come when such assurances are unnecessary.

CHAPTER I

INTRODUCTION

In the late nineteen seventies, I was a young, enthusiastic but naïve member of an evangelical Church of England congregation. Although brought up as a Christian, I had been enticed into this branch of the faith at a mission to first year students, vulnerable in a new situation, by its attractive promises of God's love for and acceptance of everyone.

It therefore came as a shock subsequently to learn from the ministry team of the church in which I'd become active that in fact God did not offer acceptance to quite everyone. Specifically, He did not accept gay people who had entered into a same-sex relationship, however loving, faithful or lifelong in intention. Apparently God required His representatives to seek out such individuals by asking outrageously personal questions, then to stigmatise them and, as far as possible, exclude them from services. A gay couple in the congregation, who had unwittingly been asked to carry the bread and wine to the altar during the offertory, were told that their contagion of the elements had "hindered the blessing" upon them and they were forbidden to play any further part in worship.

With this experience, which I found faith-challenging, began my interest in the attitudes of the Church of England towards homosexuality. A quarter of a century later, I decided to explore the possibilities of turning this interest into a research project. By coincidence, the day I went to the university to discuss the possibility of doing so was the day that the newspapers carried the announcement of the appointment of Jeffrey John as Bishop-designate of Reading. From that announcement dates the rise of the issue of homosexuality in the Church from one that had surfaced intermittently to one that has not only been constantly in the press, but has caused intense and often vitriolic discussion within the Church of England. Indeed it has become a very real threat to the unity of the Anglican Communion.

Producing a thesis deemed worthy of a doctorate turned out to be fraught with difficulty. During the time I was a research student, although my supervisor pronounced all my work to be good, examiners wanted it to be presented differently and it was necessary to rewrite several times before the thesis was passed.

However, despite these difficulties in jumping through academic hoops, the actual research process was extremely stimulating and generated material that I feel it is important should be made available to a wider readership, in the hope that it might contribute to the "listening process" in which the Church of England has long claimed to want to engage. I have therefore adapted the thesis in a way that I hope has resulted in a book accessible to all with an interest in the subject. Ironically, having spent considerable time addressing the need to present my findings in the academic style required by the university examiners, I have now done my best to reduce the academic tone so that readers will hopefully not find this off-putting. Though the written style of the book differs from that of the thesis, the substance does not.

My original intention in undertaking the project was to explore the attitudes to homosexuality that existed within the Church of England during the years 1967-2007. This period saw a complete reversal of attitudes in secular society. In 1967, homosexual acts were a criminal offence; in 2007, discrimination against homosexuals was a criminal offence. In 1967, homosexual relationships were necessarily clandestine; in 2007, they could be legally formalised in a civil partnership. By studying Church reports and a range of relevant literature I wanted to gain an overview of how different attitudes had developed during the period, but most particularly I wanted to explore these attitudes as they had affected the perceptions and experiences of selected ordained individuals.

I began by approaching retired heterosexual clergymen, selected at random from a clerical directory. As they were ordained before 1967, I felt they could contribute many interesting observations about the changing attitudes to homosexuality within both Church and society. The ten who kindly allowed me to interview them indeed had much of interest to impart, as I hope their contributions to the chapters that follow will show.

Unwittingly, their observations first drew my attention to the growth in the use of hypocrisy by the Church of England, as it has struggled against the tide of changing societal attitudes, backed by legal reforms, that affirm the right of gay people to enjoy the kind of relationships that heterosexuals take for granted. In its determination to maintain its traditional stance that same-sex expression of love is against the will of God, the Church has had to employ a range of hypocrisies, discussed in the chapters that follow. Not least of these is its continual assertion in successive reports that it wishes to "listen" to the voices of gay people. There is little evidence that, as an institution, it has seriously attempted to do so. The conclusion of its 1991 report, *Issues in Human Sexuality*, that, although same-sex relationships among lay people are just about tolerable if these people "sincerely believe it is God's call to them" (para 5.6), they are forbidden for ordained clergy, means that clergy are necessarily unlikely to come forward with their stories. Indeed, as will be shown, they are positively discouraged from doing so.

Having interviewed ten heterosexual clergymen, I then turned my attention to trying to rectify the non-existence of the long promised "listening process" by seeking gay clergymen to tell me their stories. Identifying these interviewees was less easy. There are no directories listing homosexual clergymen! Indeed, since a practising homosexual clergyman is a contradiction in terms, as officially it is not possible to be one, most of those who exist are particularly careful that they should *not* be identified. However, through personal contacts, I obtained introductions and managed to persuade twelve gay clergymen and two gay men seeking ordination to allow me to interview them. Such is the fear of exposure among gay clergy that guarantees of absolute anonymity were necessary to gain their agreement, and I felt enormously privileged that they were prepared to trust me with intensely personal and sensitive material.

Almost all the interviews were conducted in the homes of the individual interviewees. With their permission, I recorded the interviews and later transcribed them. I then sent the transcriptions to the interviewees for them to verify as accurate accounts of what they had said. The retired clergymen made very few alterations. The responses of the homosexual clergymen, however, were significantly different. In almost every case, having read the transcription, they contacted me in alarm. Having shared their stories so readily during the interview process, seeing them in print made them feel that relaxed conversation had led them to be indiscreet. It was only when they read what they had said that they realised that events, places and people of which they had spoken could lead them to be identified. Most of them asked me to edit the transcript to some degree and, sadly for my purposes, this often led to the most noteworthy details having to be disguised or cut out altogether. This in itself was indicative of the fear felt by homosexual clergy in the Church of England.

The stories the gay interviewees told of their efforts to carry out their ministries within the context of increasing negativity from the Church towards homosexual clergy led me to wonder why on earth these men persisted in working as ordained members of such an institution. If they were to obtain employment in any secular organisation, their sexuality would be of no significance. They could take their partners to social events and speak openly of their civil partnerships. They would encounter no discrimination, since the law makes this illegal. So why would they choose to work within an institution that has obtained an exemption from the Equality Act and forces them to live their domestic lives in a clandestine way?

Through analysis of the interview data, answers became clear. These gay clergymen showed enormous sympathy and respect for those in the hierarchy who feel compelled to operate the Church in what, as will become clear to anyone unfamiliar with the system, is a hypocritical way. But the most significant reason for their determination to remain within the Church emerged from the analysis to be a firm conviction in every case that they had been called by God to minister as clergymen. This absolute feeling of vocation enabled them to transcend all the hypocrisy, negativity and stigmatisation of gay clergy that they encountered in the Church's approach to them. I have termed this phenomenon the "Transcendent Vocation".

What follows are the findings from my research, presented in a way that I hope will make clear, firstly, the many forms of hypocrisy operated by the Church of England in its approach to gay clergy and, secondly, the remarkable phenomenon of the Transcendent Vocation. Chapters 3-9 are in the form generated by the content analysis that I conducted on the interview data from both the retired heterosexual clergymen and the gay clergymen. The sub-headings consist of my classification of the dimensions that emerged from the analysis, in many cases supported by a relevant quotation. Quotations from the interviews are used liberally, and it is hoped that this will lead the reader to get to know the interviewees as real people, rather than as shadowy members of a group officially considered by the Church to be sinful. In this way, I hope to contribute to a "listening process" for those willing to listen.

For reasons already explained, however, the interviewees do have to remain anonymous. I have ensured that nothing is included that could lead any one of them to be identified. Each is given a pseudonym, the initial letter of which gives the reader rudimentary information about the individual's part in the research. Names beginning with R have been given to the retired clergymen. All with this designation are heterosexual. They were ordained before 1967, had been parish priests and had obtained various levels of preferment prior to retirement. Names beginning with G have been given to the gay clergymen inter-viewed. This was an assorted group, of differing ages and ministries. Names beginning with L do not appear often, but are used for lay interviewees. The two men thus designated were seeking ordination at the time of interview.

It will be observed that all those interviewed were male. Since the rigorous process of analysing the interview data was always going to be time-consuming, I was advised early on that to include women would involve another variable that would complicate the analysis. It would have been impossible to interview women ordained during the majority of the period under discussion, since women could not be ordained as priests at all until 1994. Women priests, gay or straight, are subject to other forms of discrimination which are not part of this study.

Readers will differ in their familiarity with relevant events, developments and Church reports. In order to ensure that all can fully engage with the experiences and observations of the inter-viewees, the next chapter comprises a history of relevant signif-icant events, in order to provide the context for the study. Readers who are already fully versed in these events may like to pass over this chapter.

Following the history chapter are four chapters that provide evidence for the contention that the Church of England's approach to homosexual clergy is characterised by hypocrisy. The first of these examines the development and rise of the use of hypocrisy by the Church in its approach to homosexuals during the period 1967-2007. Taking each decade in turn, this chapter identifies several "turning points" at which the interviewees felt the situation for gay clergymen became more difficult. The second, Chapter 4, terms the gay priest an "oxymoron", namely a contradiction in terms, and explores how the Church manages to make use of the services of priests in same-sex relationships while officially forbidding them to exist. The third examines new forms of hypocrisy which the Church has felt compelled to operate since the advent of civil partnerships; and the fourth considers the hypocrisy involved in diverging so radically from the growing understanding and acceptance of different sexualities by society, even to the point of gaining an exemption from the law that forbids discrimination.

These four chapters are followed by three chapters that offer evidence for ways in which gay clergy manage to transcend all this and to wish to remain within an institution that stigmatises their lifestyle. The first of these concerns the gay interviewees' approach to the Bible. Christians who consider same-sex relationships to be sinful base their views on their belief that biblical literature condemns such relationships. In Chapter 7, the gay interviewees exemplify an attitude to the Bible which is no less respectful but does not support using a handful of verses to justify condemnation of loving relationships. By emphasising biblical principles of love and acceptance of every human being, they transcend the Church's discriminatory approach. Chapter 8 demonstrates how the gay interviewees' understanding of their sexuality as an integral part of the person God made in His image enables them to transcend traditional teaching that a homosexual orientation is a perversion.

Finally, in Chapter 9, the gay interviewees explain how they transcend the negative attitude of the Church of England, and how they maintain a fundamental love for the institution and respect for the hierarchy who perpetuate the hypocrisy previously demonstrated. The overarching reason that emerged from their interview data was their firm conviction that God had called them to serve Him by ministering as priests within the

Church of England. This "Transcendent Vocation" ensured that engaging in God's mission took priority over any concerns about the Church's attitude to homosexuality.

It is hoped that readers will approach what follows with an open mind. The findings chapters offer a valuable contribution to the listening process and it is hoped that all Christians, whatever their attitude to the issue, will indeed be prepared to listen. Listening does not of course necessarily have to lead to agreeing. However, it is hoped that readers will come to respect the interviewees' strong sense of vocation as a reason to consider whether it is indeed just in the twenty-first century to impose an outdated understanding of sexuality on people born with a homosexual orientation and to continue to stigmatise and exclude them from the Church in the name of God.

CHAPTER 2

SIGNIFICANT EVENTS AND PUBLICATIONS: 1967-2007

'Forty years' is a phrase often used in the Bible to denote a period of significance. The forty-year period 1967-2007 therefore seemed ideal for my original study. Both years ushered in important new eras for homosexuals, and there were more developments during the years in between than there had been during any similar time span in the history of the subject.

The changes in attitude that occurred in secular society during this period were enormous, with what was a criminal offence at its start being an equal opportunities issue by its close. The result within the Church was to cause substantial disagreement about how far it should stand firm in its traditional condemnation of homosexuality in view of society's growing acceptance. It will be shown in subsequent chapters how these divisions within the Church have made the lives of homosexual clergymen increasingly difficult, and how the contrast between the official Church stance and the secular developments has been the catalyst for what will be argued to be hypocrisy. This chapter outlines the events that occurred during the forty year period that are of significance. These events may well be familiar to the reader already, but it seems necessary to begin with this information in order to provide the context of the study clearly. What the interviewees said about their responses to these events can then be fully appreciated.

1. The Sexual Offences Act 1967

1967 marks the beginning of this study because it was a year of great significance for the homosexual. It is ironic that its crucial developments were largely brought about through the influence of prominent members of the Church of England, and in particular of the Archbishop of Canterbury. How decriminalisation came about is outlined below. How the events were viewed by individuals who were part of the Church at that time will be examined in Chapter 3.

In 1885, to the crime of anal intercourse, which had long been forbidden by English Criminal law, was added the crime of gross indecency. The intention of this addition had been the protection of minors. However, in practice it led to the conviction and imprisonment of hundreds of practising homosexuals. In the nineteen fifties, the relaxed wartime attitudes to sex as a whole had begun to tighten and a period of aggressive police persecution of homosexuals began, often in connection with spy scandals. Homosexuals lived in fear of police "agents provocateurs", who would try to lure them into making advances in public lavatories and then arrest them. Names were given to new sexual partners very reluctantly and love letters were written at the author's peril.

Following an article by Sherwin Bailey (1952) in which he argued that the Church had a responsibility to campaign against "this anomalous and shameful injustice", in 1954 the Church of England's Moral Welfare Council produced a report which advised that the law against male homosexual activity should be abolished. The report held that homosexual acts were certainly immoral, but the law encouraged blackmail of homosexuals and meant that they would be unwilling to seek psychological or pastoral help.

This report was a major influence in the setting up of the Wolfenden Committee, whose report in 1957 famously came to the same conclusions as that of the Moral Welfare Council. Chaired by an Anglican layman, Sir John Wolfenden, and made up of public figures, the Committee's main recommendation was that the State ought to cease making homosexual acts in private between consenting adult males a criminal offence. (Homosexual acts between women have never been a criminal offence.)

The recommendations of this report received support from several bishops of the Church of England, notably Michael Ramsey, who was at that time the Archbishop of York. Ramsey believed that physical homosexual activity was a form of lust and therefore a sin. However, he also believed that the homosexual would benefit from pastoral care, which because of the fear of prosecution he would be unlikely to seek. He expressed the hope that the government would carry out the Committee's main recommendations. However, for some years, no government was willing to bring in a bill. To do so would bring no political advantage and, although there were many people who supported reform of the law, the ordinary citizen of the country had little knowledge of the subject and the idea of homosexuality provoked disgust in many. It was not until 1964 that someone had the courage to introduce a bill into the House of Lords. This was Lord Arran, a journalist who, like all the Lords, had no constituents to affect his political future.

Michael Ramsey, now the Archbishop of Canterbury, gave his support to the bill and took a lot of trouble to encourage other bishops to do so as well, managing to persuade five or six to vote for it. He found himself attacked by various peers, one of whom accused him of contributing to pornography. Ramsey's stance was rooted in scripture and the tradition of the Church. He never asserted that homosexual acts were permissible, but he did not regret supporting the bill, which was eventually passed as the Sexual Offences Act in 1967, having passed the Commons in one overnight sitting. His opinion was based on the moral distinction between crime and sin. Coleman (1989) suggests that in the mind of ordinary people this distinction was not clear, and that Ramsey's actions meant that the Church was contributing to the new permissive society. It will be contended in Chapter 3 that in fact Ramsey's actions and the passing of the Act went unnoticed by many people, so insignificant an issue was homosexuality amongst ordinary Christians at that time.

Thus the seeds had been sown for the gradual acceptance of homosexuals that took place in society over the next decades. For now, however, there was no need for the Church to engage in the kind of double standards that emerged later.

2. The Seventies

Stephen Bates writes that "The Church of England found itself bowled along by the social changes of the 1960s, which produced unwelcome social developments" (2005:107). Certainly this period marked the beginning of the "permissive society", symptoms of which included young (and not so young) people having sex while unmarried, the rise of promiscuity, the advent of the Pill having removed the risk of pregnancy, the growth of feminism and the decline of deference towards authority and tradition. During this period and on through the seventies, single parenthood began to lose its stigma and the divorce rate began to increase. At the same time, church attendance began to decline. The Church of England was bewildered by these developments and, in order to survive, had to decide what its approach should be to these trends. In 1963, the Bishop of Woolwich, John Robinson, had published his avant-garde book, *Honest to God*, which proposed, amongst other startling new ideas, the suggestion that divorce and sexual relationships outside marriage might be acceptable. Bates sums up the dilemma by asking the question, "Should the church move slowly towards a new acceptance of different moral norms or stand out against them and preach a message that fewer and fewer people could be bothered to listen to?" (2005:108)

Gradually, the Church began to take a less rigid stance on certain issues. Baptisms of illegitimate children began to be conducted, as did marriages of couples who had been living together. Divorced people were looked upon with more sympathy, having within recent memory been excluded from polite society, and it began to look less of an impossibility for them to have remarriages blessed in church. The only sticking point for the modification of Church attitudes was homosexuality.

Now that homosexual acts were no longer illegal, it was no longer necessary for homosexual people to be so circumspect. As Norman Pittenger stated in his 1970 publication, *Time for Consent*, "Homosexuality has become a much more obvious fact in recent years than it has been in the past. In the large cities, but also in smaller communities, the presence of homosexuals, especially males, is an inescapable matter of observation" (1970:27). The Stonewall Riots of 1969 had had a knock-on effect in England. A group of New York policemen raided a bar, the Stonewall Inn, known for being frequented by gay people. This was a matter of routine, but this time the people concerned did not submit meekly, as usually happened, and the ensuing disturbances came to be known as the Stonewall Riots. These further fuelled many homosexuals' desire and courage to "come out".

In the Church, it continued to be necessary to be cautious about letting one's sexuality be known, particularly if one were a clergyman. Colin Buchanan in a chapter of his book, *Taking the Long View*, describes and discusses the developments of the seventies. As a theological college principal and later a bishop, Buchanan was himself involved in many of the decisions and discussions which he outlines. Buchanan confides that, in the latter part of the sixties, Mervyn Stockwood, who was latterly Bishop of Southwark and is now known to have been homosexual, in orientation at least, told him that he advised young clergymen not to do anything they would not like him to know about, but that, if they must do it, they should do it north of the Thames. Hinting of the double standards to come, Buchanan suggests that this "opened an official connivance which contained the sparks of a revolution" (2006:199).

Some theological colleges in the seventies began to accept

ordinands to whose sexuality they turned a blind eye. Despite the fact that the official line remained that all homosexual activity was forbidden as sinful, unofficially parts of the Church were acting as though this was no longer the case. Double standards had certainly come into force and concern about this was expressed by some theological college principals. As a result of their concern, a working party was set up by the Board of Social Responsibility, chaired by John Yates, the Bishop of Gloucester. Their report was published in 1979.

Meanwhile the Lambeth Conference of 1978 passed a resolution that for the first time recognised the existence of homosexuals and the dilemmas faced by the church in the light of their increased profile. Resolution 10, entitled "Human Relationships and Sexuality", re-affirmed heterosexuality as the scriptural norm, but recognised "the need for deep and dispassionate study of the question of homosexuality, which would take seriously both the teaching of Scripture and the results of scientific and medical research". It seemed that the way was paved for a reappraisal of the traditional blanket condemnation, but even thirty years later little change had occurred.

The report of the working party led by the Bishop of Gloucester finished its thorough report in July 1978. By that time, more conservative members had been appointed to the Board of Social Responsibility and, when they looked at the report, they decided it was too liberal. Known as "The Gloucester Report", it examined the relevant biblical passages, discussed causes of homosexual behaviour in the light of recent scientific claims that not everyone is capable of a heterosexual response, and advocated pastoral concern for those who are not, acknowledging that homosexuals find themselves in a situation of great difficulty through no fault of their own. The working party stated that it did not accept the claim that homosexual relationships are equal to heterosexual ones, but that it believed homosexuals should be freed from the pressure either to pass as heterosexuals or to commit entirely to a heterosexual culture. It concluded that there was no good reason for stigmatising people who had in good conscience entered into a stable same-sex partnership. Gay Christians viewed the Report as hopeful for the future.

In Colin Buchanan's reference to the discussion of the Report at the 1979 Synod, he describes how he directed a question to Graham Leonard, the chairman of the Board, about what official guidance for theological college principals regarding the approach they should take to homosexual ordinands it in fact contained. Leonard replied that it was up to theological college principals to say what they thought. Buchanan expresses the irony of the situation: "So, nearly six years on from the request, with an actual (if ambivalent) report in front of us, we were being told we might as well have made up our own minds in the first place" (2006:202)

It should by now be becoming apparent how the dilemma caused by the growing acceptance of homosexuality by society since 1967 was beginning to be met by the practice of "turning a blind eye" in the absence of any agreement about a definitive policy about the issue. This practice gradually developed into the hypocritical approach that was rife twenty years later.

3. The Eighties

Writing at the end of the decade, Peter Coleman bemoans that the eighties had proved disappointing to those who hoped at the beginning that the Gloucester Report "would inaugurate a more courteous era for gay Christians" (1989:180). A further debate on the Report in 1981 was inconclusive and it was never endorsed by the Church.

The uncertainty felt by the theological college principals was still unresolved. Colin Buchanan reports that, when he asked again at the 1984 Synod whether the House of Bishops planned to issue guidance about the acceptability of practising homosexuals for ordination, Robert Runcie, the Archbishop of

Canterbury, merely replied that "guidance is best given in particular cases" (2006:203). In other words, the official policy stood, but unofficially it could be ignored: double standards indeed.

The 1986 "Osborne Report" was never published. The House of Bishops judged it to be too liberal and it was suppressed. Only 22 years later was it possible for the public to read it, when the Church Times published it in its entirety on its website. The Report suggests that all homosexual acts cannot be judged as morally identical and advises that the Church should be more welcoming to gay people. How different things might be today if it had been published in 1986!

Before the Osborne Report was completed, however, a very significant debate took place in Synod, which was to do much to thwart those who hoped that the Church's attitude to homosexuals was becoming more liberal.

Newly elected evangelical member of Synod, Tony Higton, the Rector of Hawkwell in Essex, tabled a Private Member's Motion calling for the Church to reaffirm its commitment to the biblical standards of sexual intercourse taking place only between a man and a woman who were married to each other and of the sinfulness of homosexual acts in all circumstances. Amendments by Michael Baughen, Bishop of Chester, and Peter Forster, representing Durham and Newcastle Universities, stated that homosexual genital acts (as well as fornication and adultery) fall short of the ideal of sexual intercourse as an act of total commitment within marriage, and proposed that these should be "met by a call to repentance and the exercise of compassion".

This was a motion that, as Bates puts it, "struck at the heart of the moral panic gathering about the nation about the emerging worldwide AIDS epidemic" (2005:115). HIV/AIDS had arrived in England in the mid-eighties. There was at that time no effective treatment and it was always fatal. Although not all sufferers had contracted the disease through homosexual acts, publicity was such that AIDS had become known as the "gay plague". The resulting fear of homosexuals and general ignorance about how HIV/AIDS could be passed on had caused a public attitude which meant the attack on homosexuality in the Higton motion was the part of it that attracted attention.

The "Higton Debate", as it came to be called, was exactly the sort of discussion that the hierarchy sought to avoid, since it was the direct opposite of their unofficial policy not to inquire too deeply about the lifestyles of those they chose to ordain. However, the motion received wide support among the lay members of the Synod as well as from evangelical clergy. This was not only because of the concern about AIDS but also because, nearly fourteen years after the request of the theological principals' conference, there had still been no official guidance from the House of Bishops and homosexuals were still being selected for ordination.

The debate could not be avoided and, on November 11th 1987, the amended motion was passed 403-8, with 15 abstentions. This was a milestone in the recent history of the issue, putting a stop to the liberal agenda and providing the Church of England with the official condemnation of the acceptance of unrepentant homosexuals which it had so far lacked. In 2003, *Some Issues in Human Sexuality* declared that this debate was a way in which the "mind of the Church came to be expressed" (para 1.3.16), although it was clearly not the mind of the whole Church. The significance of the Higton Debate in the lives of homosexual clergymen will be examined in Chapter 3.

The 1988 Lambeth Conference added nothing to the issue, Resolution 64 merely reaffirming the statement of the 1978 Conference. Thus ended the decade which had begun so hopefully for homosexual Christians.

4. The Nineties
The nineties began with the publication of the key report, *Issues*

in Human Sexuality. Published in December 1991, this was the product of the House of Bishops' intention to create a policy statement on the Church's pastoral and theological position on sexual matters, mainly those relating to homosexuality. It is a crucial work in relation to this study, since much of the hypocrisy contended to be in the Church's attitude to homosexuals is based around its contents.

The booklet begins with a presentation of the situation in the Church of England at that time, summing up the reports and statements mentioned above. There follows a discussion of the passages in the Bible concerned with sexuality, ending with "The Christian Vision for Human Sexuality". This vision is that, because sexual love is a wonderful gift from God, through this a man and a woman can be united in a relationship that helps them to mature as individuals. Their partnership is a blessing to the whole community and forms the stable and loving environment in which children need to be brought up.

The next section proceeds to explain that the "Phenomenon of Homosexual Love" falls short of this vision. Rather strangely, the authors of the report decided to use the term "homophile" to refer to people "who feel erotic love for someone of the same sex". They explain that they have chosen to use this terminology "because it is as yet free from some of the negative overtones attaching to the term 'homosexual', and because it can help to avoid clumsy circumlocutions in referring to same-sex love" (para 4.1).

Issues concludes that, while a "homophile" way of life cannot be commended "as in itself as faithful a reflection of God's purposes as the heterophile", it does "not reject those who sincerely believe it is God's call to them". Homosexuals are valued by God and their partnerships can be a blessing both to them and to their communities. The report commends them to a life of abstinence, but suggests that, if they find this impossible, in some circumstances "a loving and faithful homophile partnership in intention lifelong, where mutual self-giving includes the physical expression of their attachment" can be accepted for lay members of the Church (para 5.6).

However, this conclusion does not extend to members of the clergy or candidates for ordination. For them, this way of life is not acceptable, since their lives "must be free of anything which will make it difficult for others to have confidence in them" (para 5.14). Despite some critics defending the expectation of higher moral standards from the clergy as being proper and appropriate, this "two-tier" discipline has caused strong feelings in many as representing a double standard.

The report then goes on to address the possible assumption that bishops should be more rigorous in searching out and exposing clergy who are engaging in sexually active homophile relationships. This approach is rejected for two reasons. The first is that to assume that two people of the same sex who are sharing a home necessarily have a sexual relationship is considered to be "a grossly unfair assumption". The second is that a general inquisition into the lives of the clergy would infringe their right to privacy, indicate an inappropriate distrust and undermine their morale. Although the Church must take steps to avoid public scandal and to protect its teaching, bishops will treat their clergy with trust and respect if they cause no scandal, and express the hope that all Christians will do the same. This policy, which might be regarded with gratitude by those affected by the report's conclusions, is generally summed up disparagingly in the phrase, "don't ask, don't tell." In other words, the Church of England is happy to turn a blind eye to homosexual conduct among the clergy, so long as no public scandal results.

Issues in Human Sexuality was not laid before the Synod and, in the Preface, Archbishop George Carey introduced the report by saying that it was not expected to be the last word on the subject. Nevertheless, it became a way of stating a common approach by bishops to ordination questions and has since been widely taken to be the official view of the Church of England. It has become customary for clergymen being elevated to higher positions within the Church publicly to state their adherence to the position on sexuality expressed in *Issues*.

Six years after the publication of *Issues in Human Sexuality*, a Southwark archdeacon, David Gerrard, seeing that the House of Bishops was not bringing the report before the Synod, tabled a private member's motion which led to the report finally being debated. That such debate had not taken place before was due to nervousness about a topic which by now was beginning to arouse very strong feelings amongst those of differing theological positions. The result of Gerrard's motion was that the Synod officially supported *Issues'* recommendation of further study and discussion.

In 1998, bishops from the Anglican Communion across the world met yet again for the ten-yearly Lambeth Conference. This time, feelings about homosexuality ran much higher than in the previous two conferences where it had been discussed. The approach between conservative African bishops and liberal American bishops was confrontational before the Conference even convened. A sub-group studying human sexuality was unable to reach a common mind on the scriptural, theological and scientific issues and there was fierce debate in the full Conference, which finally drew up Resolution I.10.

This resolution has become an important backdrop to all discussions on homosexuality since. It stated the belief of the Conference that "abstinence is right for those who are not called to marriage", and its recognition that "there are among us persons who experience themselves as having a homosexual orientation". Such people were assured "that they are loved by God and that all baptised, believing and faithful persons, regardless of sexual orientation, are full members of the Body of Christ". However, homosexual practice was rejected as "incompatible with Scripture", although the Resolution called for sensitive pastoral ministry to all "irrespective of sexual orientation" and condemnation of "irrational fear of homosexuals". The Conference also stated that it could not "advise the legitimising or blessing of same-sex unions nor ordaining those involved in same gender unions". It did, however, commit itself to "listen to the experience of homosexual persons". As has already been contended, very little such listening has since taken place, which is an omission this study seeks to redress.

The Resolution was carried by 526-70, with 45 abstentions, but afterwards 146 bishops, including some of those who had voted for it, signed a statement in which they apologised to homosexual Christians for any sense of rejection that had been brought about by the Resolution. They also expressed regret that the voices of homosexuals had not been heard in the discussion. Forty-two English bishops were among the signatories.

Lambeth Resolution I.10 is, like all Lambeth Conference decisions, purely advisory. Nevertheless, just as the conclusions of *Issues in Human Sexuality* have been considered to be the established policy of the Church of England, it has been generally taken ever since to be the established policy of all churches within the Anglican Communion.

These two important documents, produced during the nineties, were of crucial importance in the events of the next decade which, in the absence of an obvious abbreviation, will be termed the "noughties". Their significance in the lives of homosexual clergymen will be explored in later chapters.

5. The Noughties

The Church of England and Anglican Communion had been steered through the nineties by the evangelical Archbishop of Canterbury, George Carey. In 2002, he announced that he would retire in November. In July, his successor was announced as the Bishop of Monmouth and Archbishop of the Church in Wales, Rowan Williams.

From the moment he was known to be a candidate, the evangelical wing of the Church began to express feelings that ranged from concern through grave reservations to hostility. Rowan Williams was an Anglo-Catholic who was closely associated with the organisation Affirming Catholicism, but this was not the primary cause of evangelicals' anxiety. What alarmed them was that he was known to be sympathetic to the cause of homosexuals within the Church of England and, in particular, to that of homosexual clergy.

Notably, Williams had given the Michael Harding Address in 1989. This is named in honour of the late partner of Richard Kirker, the founder of the Lesbian and Gay Christian Movement. Later published as *The Body's Grace*, the address argued that celibacy was not the only ethically acceptable lifestyle for a homosexual. Addressing the traditional concern that sexual activity should primarily be for the procreation of children, he suggested that neither Jesus nor St Paul spoke of marriage as being only for this purpose. He went on to assert that, since the Church now accepted contraception, condemnation of all same-sex relationships must rely on a fundamentalist acceptance of "a number of very ambiguous texts" or on an insistence on the importance of physical differences in the genders "without regard to psychological structures" (2002:12).

When this was first published, there was as yet no *Issues* to suggest that such an assertion was unwise for someone expected to advance in the Church. Moreover, Williams was at that time primarily an academic, and preferment or being a public figure were not yet an obvious concern.

A later work, written in 1997, post-*Issues* and while Williams was Bishop of Monmouth, was an essay contributed to a publication produced in response to the "St Andrew's Day Statement". In this, he raises many questions about whether homosexually active partnerships need always be considered wrong. For example, "if you do not accept that homosexual desire is itself a mark of disorder, can you confidently say that the presence of this desire must always be a sign that sexual expression is ruled out?" (2003:18).

Evangelicals were extremely concerned by the lack of theological orthodoxy and unsound approach to the Gospel that Rowan Williams was seen to have demonstrated. Various groups were vociferous in their antipathy to his appointment as Archbishop of Canterbury. Liberal Anglicans, on the other hand, were delighted by Rowan Williams' appointment. Homosexual members of the Church, and homosexual clergy in particular, looked forward to his archiepiscopacy as a time when the conservative policies of the nineties might be overturned and when open acceptance for homosexuals might be ushered in.

Both liberals and conservatives, however, had not reckoned with an important element of Williams' theology. He did not see the position of Archbishop as being a platform from which he could put forward his own views and practice. On the contrary, he saw his task now as that of holding the Anglican Communion together, reconciling rather than aggravating different theologies. Although he never denied the views he had expressed in his earlier writings, he did what he could to try to pacify his opponents. Most notably, he wrote to each Primate in the Communion to say that he saw the Lambeth resolution as highly significant and he also wrote to the bishops in the Church of England to say that, whatever his own views, he intended to uphold the policy expressed in *Issues*. Although done from principled motives, this was the beginning of Williams' contribution to hypocrisy in the Church.

With the conservative evangelicals' mistrust of Rowan Williams and the liberal wing's hopes for tolerance of homosexuals being ushered in with his archiepiscopacy, the stage was set for the momentous events of 2003.

The headlines on May 20th 2003 fulfilled the wildest dreams of gay Christians. Dr Jeffrey John, Canon Chancellor at

Southwark Cathedral, was to be the next Bishop of Reading, one of the area bishops in the diocese of Oxford. He had been nominated by the Bishop of Oxford, Richard Harries, who had originally thought of John because he had ideal credentials for the position. Not only was he a very able theologian, but he fitted Harries' wish for an Anglo-Catholic with a heart for mission.

However, despite these credentials, Harries at first ruled John out because of his well-known views about homosexuality. These were well documented. Most notably, Jeffrey John had written a book entitled *Permanent, Faithful, Stable,* the title being taken from a phrase in the Gloucester Report to describe the kind of homosexual partnerships that might be considered acceptable. John begins the introduction to his book by stating that his aim is to argue that "homosexual relationships should be accepted and blessed by the Church, provided that the quality and commitment of the relationship are the same as those expected of a Christian marriage" (2000:1). He ends his introduction by asserting that the Church has a duty to offer homosexuals in this kind of relationship the same kind of support as it offers to heterosexual couples in marriage.

Amongst his other writings and lectures on the same theme was Jeffrey John's contribution to *The Way Forward,* mentioned above as a response to the St Andrew's Day Statement. This paragraph illustrates a key argument of *Transcendent Vocation*:

"For a Christian homosexual, as for the Christian hetero-sexual, the question is always, 'What for me is the way of holiness? How is God calling me to fulfil the purpose of my creation, to grow in love and self-sacrifice, and so in his image?' To find the answer to that question in a call to a faithful, lifelong, same-sex partnership (and let me be clear that I am defending no other kind of homosexual practice) is no more or less self-indulgent than finding it in a call to marriage or celibacy." (2003:46)

In addition, it was well known in clergy circles that John was himself a homosexual. Colin Buchanan knew him when they worked together in Woolwich and writes that Jeffrey John openly acknowledged that he had met his homosexual partner while a student at St Stephen's House in Oxford twenty years previously and that they had been together ever since.

Although Richard Harries had originally discounted John as Bishop of Reading, he was persuaded to think again by the Dean of Southwark, Colin Slee, who sent him a lengthy reference he had prepared when John had been a strong candidate to succeed Rowan Williams at Monmouth. In his biography of Harries, John Peart-Binns (2007) alleges that Harries telephoned Rowan Williams twice to ask if he would be prepared to consecrate Jeffrey John, and on both occasions Williams said that he would.

As soon as Jeffrey John's appointment was announced, the floodgates of opposition opened. Michael Hampson, in his cynically titled book, *Last Rites: The End of the Church of England* suggests that the evangelical wing of the Church was still angry about its failure to prevent Williams' appointment: "All the resentment and bitterness surrounding that failure was poured into the new campaign against Jeffrey John" (2006:129).

The facts that John had admitted not only to being homosexual but also to being in a long-term relationship made him totally unsuitable to be a bishop, said evangelicals. Moreover, he was known to have criticised both the 1998 Lambeth Resolution and the hypocrisy of the double standards for laity and clergy expressed in *Issues in Human Sexuality*. How could someone be appointed to a position where he would be expected to uphold a policy that he had denounced, particularly since he was defying that policy in his private life?

His opponents were unimpressed that John had been required to give an assurance about his lifestyle and had stated that, although he had a long-standing male partner, the relationship had been celibate for more than a decade. Nor were they convinced by a statement he had given in which he said that the role of a bishop was to uphold the doctrine of the Church, rather than his personal opinions. He pledged in the statement that he would therefore uphold the teaching on sexuality set out in *Issues*. Here John was in effect expressing his own willingness to enter into the prevalent hypocrisy.

Meetings, statements and official letters were abundant during June. A significant number of clergy in the Oxford diocese and a significant number of bishops refused to recognise not only Jeffrey John's authority if he was consecrated but also the authority of any other bishop who supported him. Rowan Williams found himself in an impossible position. Having largely weathered the original opposition to his own appointment the previous year, his judgment in appointing Jeffrey John as Bishop of Reading was now being so severely questioned and criticised that confidence in his archiepiscopate was lower than ever and it was vital to rectify this.

Peart-Binns tells us that, when Richard Harries was summoned to Lambeth Palace on July 5th, he thought that the meeting was to discuss how best the issue could be handled. In fact, it was so that the Archbishop could tell him that he had decided not to go through with the nomination. Jeffrey John was persuaded to issue a statement saying, not that the Archbishop was unprepared to consecrate him, but that he had himself decided to withdraw because of the divisive nature of the appointment. The most blatant and public example of the hypocrisy of the Church hierarchy, the significance of this episode in the lives of homosexual clergymen will be examined in Chapter 3.

The crisis in the Church of England seemed to have been averted, but soon a greater one threatened the entire Anglican Communion. A month after Jeffrey John's withdrawal, the Episcopal Church in the USA (ECUSA) announced the election of Gene Robinson as the next Bishop of New Hampshire. Robinson had been married and divorced, but more significantly he was openly gay and living with his male partner. There was no suggestion that this relationship was celibate.

This triggered a crisis in the Anglican Communion. In October, Rowan Williams invited the Primates to an emergency meeting in London. This led to the setting up of the Lambeth Commission, which was given the mandate to report on the legal and theological implications of ECUSA's action and to include practical recommendations for maintaining communion within and between the churches of the Anglican Communion in the light of this action. The consecration of the openly gay Gene Robinson, unlike that of the celibate Jeffrey John, went ahead.

In November 2003, *Some Issues in Human Sexuality; A Guide to the Debate* was published by the House of Bishops. Very much longer than its predecessor, Bishop Richard Harries' Foreword explains that its function was a guide to the debate on questions that had arisen in response to *Issues* since 1991. It was intended to clarify what the earlier report had said, and not to indicate any change in the position of the House of Bishops on the matter of the acceptability of same-sex relationships.

Accordingly, although it covers a considerable amount of material very thoroughly, with chapters outlining, for example, the current debate, the use of the Bible in sexual ethics, the theology of sexuality, homosexuals in the life of the church and handling some current controversies in the Church, it does not come to any new conclusions. As with so many reports and statements about homosexuality, further prayer and study are recommended.

On October 18th 2004, the report of the Lambeth Commission was published. Called "The Windsor Report", the 121-page document stated that the commission had not been invited, and was not intending to comment either on the ethics of same-sex relationships or on the suitability of practising homosexuals for ordination as priests or consecration as bishops. However, it stressed the importance of recognising the difficulties being caused by the radically different positions being sincerely held on the issue in different parts of the Anglican Communion. In order to try to forestall further crises caused by individual churches acting in contradiction to accepted practice, it recommended that a covenant should be drawn up and accepted by each province of the Anglican Communion, which would set out an agreed understanding of Anglican discipline.

Meanwhile, society's attitude to homosexuality was becoming ever more tolerant, and on December 5th 2005 the Civil Partnership Act came into force, making it possible for the first time for same-sex couples to obtain the same legal rights as married couples by registering a civil partnership. In anticipation of this, the House of Bishops issued a Pastoral Statement on July 25th, in order to "help the Church as it addresses the pastoral and other implications of the new legislation".

The Pastoral Statement emphasised that the new legislation made no change to the law of the land in relation to marriage, which remained that marriage could be entered into only by a man and a woman. It pointed out that the legislation left open the nature of the commitment that members of a couple chose to make to each other, and that it should not be assumed that those entering a civil partnership were necessarily engaged in a sexual relationship.

The Statement went on to make clear that the Church's teaching on sexual ethics remained unchanged, namely that the proper context for sexual activity was still considered to be solely within marriage. The Church would, nevertheless, minister "sensitively and pastorally to those Christians who conscientiously decide to order their lives differently". However, services of blessing for those registering a civil partnership were not to be permitted.

As far as clergy were concerned, entering a civil partnership would not be regarded as "intrinsically incompatible with holy orders". However, ordained people intending to do so must expect to be asked to give their bishop an assurance that "the relationship is consistent with the standards for the clergy set out in *Issues in Human Sexuality*", in other words that it was not sexual. Not only is this another example of double standards for clergy and laity, but it will be contended in Chapter 5 that, as a further example of hypocrisy, the expectation expressed in this statement is rarely adhered to.

In a further move towards the full acceptance of homosexuals by society, in 2007 the Equality Act (Sexual Orientation) Regulations came into force in England. This made it unlawful for homosexual people to be discriminated against in the provision of goods, facilities and services. Religious organisa-tions were, however, exempt from these regulations. Thus the Church of England, which, based on its claims to follow the teachings of Jesus Christ who welcomed those on the margins of society, should be championing human rights, is one of the few organisations legally permitted to discriminate against homosexuals.

So ended the period covered by this study. In society, the change in attitudes to homosexuality during the forty years can be summed up in the title of Stephen Cretney's book, *From Odious Crime to Gay Marriage*. At the beginning of 1967, to engage in homosexual acts was indeed an imprisonable crime; in 2007, it was made a crime to discriminate against those who did so. Moreover, although civil partnerships were not described as marriage in the Civil Partnership Act, the media were describing the first ceremonies, notably that of the singer Elton John, as "weddings" from the start.

"In little more than fifty years, behaviour regarded as *criminal*....has been moved not merely into the neutral zone where the state leaves it to the individual to make decisions but into the zone in which the state, by creating legal or administrative structures, recognizes and approves the conduct in question." (Cretney 2006:2)

In the Church of England, however, the behaviour in question had certainly not been officially moved into such a zone by 2007, and nor has it by the present day. The strong conviction of some of its members that it should be and the equally strong conviction of others that it should not has prompted a crisis that has escalated to such proportions that it has threatened to split the Church. For an institution based on the life of someone who taught his followers to love one another, who mixed freely with those on the margins of society and emphasised the importance of justice, the strife over this issue must in itself be hypocritical. Those at its heart, clergymen in homosexual relationships, could today escape all the negativity with which they are faced if they moved into wholly secular employment. The reasons that they do not do so are the focus of this book.

CHAPTER 3

FORTY YEARS OF TURNING POINTS

In outlining the developments that took place during the period 1967-2007, Chapter 2 showed that, as the period progressed, the Church of England was forced to make increasing use of hypocrisy. In the face of increasing acceptance of sexual diversity by society, this was made necessary by the hierarchy's determination to maintain that heterosexual relationships only are at the heart of the divine plan, and in order to justify its continued policy of marginalizing homosexuals. Significantly, by the end of the period, such an attitude had become so out of step with society that the Church was granted permission to discriminate in a way that in secular situations is now illegal.

Chapter 3 is the first of four chapters which seek to offer further demonstration and explanation of this hypocrisy. They do so primarily by presenting extracts from the interviews with the clergymen who agreed to take part in my original research project. The extracts represent actual lived experiences of people who witnessed or were personally affected by the developments and issues discussed.

Beginning with the passing of the Sexual Offences Act in 1967, this chapter moves through the decades, presenting and discussing relevant experiences of the interviewees, as well as their observations. Through this discussion, the chapter not only offers further illustration of the growth of the hypocrisy operated by the Church, but also highlights a number of events as turning points in this process. The inclusion of data from the retired heterosexual clergymen, whose ministries spanned all the events discussed, adds further to the understanding of how the hypocrisy developed. Moreover, the chapter gives an insight into how each of the turning points identified increased the tension felt by the homosexual clergymen as they strove to maintain their position within an institution that was, officially at least, increasingly anti-gay.

Each sub-heading in this and all the chapters that follow has been chosen to represent a "dimension" or theme that emerged during the lengthy process of analysing the interview data. Quotations from the interviews are used liberally to illustrate the dimensions discussed. Not only do these quotations give the reader a clear and often moving insight into real-life experiences and beliefs, but they allow the actual voices of the interviewees to be heard. In the case of the homosexual interviewees, it is a rare chance to hear the voices of gay clergy in the way that the Church has often claimed to wish to do. Sometimes contributions from more than one interviewee are presented in the same paragraph. It should be stressed that this does not mean the interviewees were in conversation with each other; every interview was conducted individually. Linking contributions in this way (and often without the paragraph breaks that are the convention in reporting speech) is intended to give emphasis to the points made.

As explained in Chapter 1, all the interviewees are given pseudonyms to protect their anonymity. The initial letter of each pseudonym shows the reader the part played by that interviewee in the research process. The method adopted is described again here as a reminder: Names beginning with R are given to the retired heterosexual clergymen, all of whom had been ordained before the passing of the Sexual Offences Act in 1967 and who represent a generation brought up to believe unequivocally that homosexual relationships were wrong. Names beginning with G are given to the gay clergymen interviewed. These men were of differing ages and were serving in differing ministries. Names beginning with L are given to two gay men who were seeking ordination at the time of their interview and were therefore still laymen.

The 1967 decriminalisation of homosexuality, or "We didn't know anything about it"

The passing of the Sexual Offences Act in 1967 was of enormous significance. It freed homosexuals from the constant fear that their liaisons and relationships would be discovered and punished with imprisonment. It marked the beginning of the end to furtiveness and shame, and the start of what would become movements campaigning for gay liberation and equality. As Michael Ramsey, the Archbishop of Canterbury, had been instrumental in achieving the passing of the Act, it seemed logical to think that clergymen who were in ministry at the time must have some opinion about the appropriateness of Archbishop Ramsey's support, and that they would be able to give some idea of the feelings of ordinary church members of the time. However, all but one denied having had any knowledge of this highly significant Act being passed at all, let alone of the Archbishop's part in the process.

The only one of the ten retired interviewees who acknowledged any memory of the Act was Robert, who stated that, although prior to the Act homosexuals had to be very circumspect, he was always aware of their existence. When he was doing National Service during the early fifties, he was solicited in the showers; and later in the decade, at theological college, he recognised *"three or four"* of the 65 students as being homosexual. He declared that *"anybody who says, 'Oh no, I didn't know anything about that' must walk round with their eyes and ears shut!"* Nevertheless, all the other retired interviewees said just that.

They gave various reasons for their lack of knowledge. Ronald felt the subject of homosexuality was a taboo: *"Like cancer, it was something you didn't mention."* Several said that homosexuality was not on their "agenda" at that time. Most were curates then and concerned with a range of other issues. Different priorities of the time were mentioned: for example, the debate about the Anglican Methodist Union, which Ralph felt had taken up many people's attention rather than the decriminalisation. And Robin said that a much more commonly encountered problem was unmarried girls becoming pregnant, such as was the daughter of a distressed member of his Church Council: *"That was where we were on sexual matters at that time, I think. Certainly where I was."*

The experience of homosexuals recounted by the retired interviewees was very limited, and particularly during the sixties. Roy felt that he *"probably had a very naïve life I think, but I'm not sure at that age and also not within the church where I would never have dreamt of meeting anybody."* Others too felt they had either never met a homosexual or at least not one they recognised as such at that time. What experience they had had was limited to the 'sleazy'. The choirmaster at Robin's church had been *"in trouble... Well that was what these days would be called paedophilia, choirboys, you know."* Robin also remembered being warned about *"people doing funny things in public lavatories"* when he left theological college.

Almost without exception, none of these men could remember the issue being discussed either by clergy or parishioners. *"I don't remember it being brought up in the parish, or anybody being particularly concerned about it at all. I can't remember it ever cropping up. Nor do I remember homosexuality being an issue,"* said Roland. Robin wondered whether the situation might have been different in inner city areas. No one had been faced with a pastoral situation where homosexuality had been a factor, which is not surprising when it was a criminal offence, but they had not at any time in the years after 1967 either.

When I sent a draft copy of this dimension to Roy, he commented that it was unremarkable that these interviewees had been oblivious to the passing of the Sexual Offences Act, since it had not affected them. Roderick's statement leads on from this: *"I may not have been alert to [the Act's] significance, though perhaps it opened the door to the changes in social attitudes which have led to the questions that you are now asking. The fact is that I was unaware of it. I am fascinated to realise this!"*

Thus this dimension illustrates the experience and attitudes of those in ministry at the beginning of the period of the study, together with the obliviousness of ordinary people at that time to the presence of homosexuals among them. Such disinterestedness enabled Michael Ramsey to be true to his own principles in supporting the decriminalisation of homosexuality without the fear of media attention or outcry amongst conservative Christians that have accompanied Rowan Williams' attempts to advocate inclusiveness. The question of hypocrisy does not arise at this point, since the attitude of the Church to homosexuality was in line with that of society.

What a difference an Act makes, or "It was easier before it became legal"

The responses of the homosexual clergymen corroborate the lack of awareness of the retired interviewees. A few of the homosexuals interviewed were of an age to remember the passing of the Sexual Offences Act. Those who were not were able to contribute valuable thoughts gained through talking to older homosexuals and from reading about the period. The analysis of these responses generated two clearly complementary themes: "Pre-1967: unacceptable in society but tacitly accepted in the Church", and "Post-1967: incipiently acceptable in society but unaccepted in the Church".

"People say to me, 'It never happened in our day,' and I say, 'Well, of course it happened. You just never spoke about it', said Grant. Because homosexual acts were illegal before 1967, there was very little way in which they would be brought to the attention of ordinary people, hence the lack of awareness of the retired respondents. This lack of general awareness conversely made it easier for homosexual clergymen to conduct relationships without attracting attention. Grant went on: *"I have spoken to older*

clergy in the past about when they lived and had relationships in the time before that. And one of them was saying to me that it was almost, within certain sections of the Church, it was a bit like Brideshead Revisited. There was a sort of tolerance among people in the Oxbridge circle, like a gentleman's club. And in a sense it was easier then before it became legal. He said you just got on with your life; nobody knew if you had a partner."

There were certain influential clergymen at that time who are now known to have been homosexual and who gave support and encouragement to younger homosexuals wishing to be ordained. Gerald was advised to go and see the theologian, the Revd. Harry Williams, who was his tutor at Cambridge. *"And at university I did go through a sort of crisis of, you know, was I then gay? And could I go on and be ordained, and what was I going to do about it? And Harry really saw me through that. He was very upfront about his own sexuality. He was very open with undergraduates who were his friends."* Harry Williams subsequently wrote frankly about his own homosexuality in his autobiography (1982).

Gerald also received support from Mervyn Stockwood, *"who knew my parents and himself was gay, though much less open about it. And I don't believe he – you know, I believe he was a celibate. He was often criticised for not being, on very little evidence. But I think it was more that he was a controversial figure. But he knew that I was gay and said, when he was made Bishop of Southwark, 'If you can get yourself trained, I will ordain you'."* In retirement, Stockwood wrote about his feelings about gay partnerships in a letter to a priest whom he knew to have been conducting same-sex blessings: "…as you know, I did a lot to help in this matter during my episcopate, but I never appeared in print or joined a campaign" (Bates 2005:300).

Thus, prior to 1967, gay clergy would not have expected their sexuality to be tolerated in the Church while it was not tolerated by society. After the passing of the Sexual Offences Act, however, the situation was reversed. Homosexuality gradually began to become acceptable in society, but it was not officially accepted in the Church. The older gay subjects agreed that the Act did not have any direct effect on the Church, as the sinfulness of homosexuality was never questioned. *"What it did was that it began to change social attitudes,"* observed Gerald. Gus recalled, *"I was just overjoyed that people were not hounded in their own homes or in public lavatories and things. I was rejoicing like so many other people that times had changed."* To the subsequent question, "Do you think it made any difference in the Church?" he replied, *"No I don't think it did really. I mean, even now, I can't believe it that the Church is so homophobic."* As the Church strove to maintain ethical standards that were beginning to be considered outdated by society, the need for hypocrisy had begun.

The Seventies – Liberality creeping in

Graham agreed that, socially, things were easier for homosexuals after the 1967 Act, but that *"whether they were in the Church is another matter. I think it was still a hidden subject. You didn't really talk about it. Best not to talk about it at all."* It was not necessary to talk about it because homosexuality was not an issue at that time. *"People didn't look for it. They weren't aware of it. It was a very different climate altogether,"* explained George.

Because of this, it was relatively easy for homosexuals to be accepted for ordination if they fulfilled the necessary criteria. Candidates were not asked about their sexuality when going through the selection process. Giles was doing so during this period and, when asked whether he had been open about his sexuality, he replied, *"No, because it wasn't an issue then, and I have to say I think, although I was aware of it myself, I wouldn't have articulated it in that sort of way. Certainly in those days, it wasn't a time when if a) you were a Christian and b) you were a candidate for the ministry, I think if you went around articulating your sexuality you'd probably be sent to the back of the queue."*

Records were much more informal at that time, Roy told me. When clergy moved from one parish to another, they would do so with an informal recommendation from their superior rather than an official report. Graham explained, *"They didn't interview you so much in those days."* His bishop had not known of his gay involvement when he appointed him to a new post.

However, increasingly homosexuals were being selected by bishops and theological colleges who were aware of these candidates' sexuality. Several interviewees knew of examples of this happening, and indeed it was because the principals of theological colleges were concerned about the situation and wanted guidance that the Gloucester Report was commissioned. The gay respondents who had been at theological college during the seventies confirmed that they had been part of a group of other homosexual ordinands. *"When I went to college I found there were others of similar orientation,"* said George. Greg claimed that Robert Runcie was *"gay-sympathetic"* when he was a bishop. He was prepared to ordain Richard Kirker, who started the Gay Christian Movement. However, as Greg explained, and is corroborated by Stephen Bates (2005), the reason Kirker was never priested was that he openly challenged Runcie *"on the gay issue"* when he became Archbishop of Canterbury. In other words, liberality was creeping in, but it was furtive and unofficial.

Graham summed up the situation during the seventies thus: *"I suppose it was more liberal. What set it all back of course in the gay world was HIV and AIDS. Just at the time when you thought gay people would be accepted more, they were seen as dirty and filthy people who get terminal illnesses by their sex."* In other words, it had been hoped by homosexuals that the unofficially liberal attitude being adopted in some parts of the Church would be endorsed by the House of Bishops, particularly considering the liberal conclusions of the Gloucester Report. Such hopes were to be disappointed, however, as the events of the eighties led to more deeply ingrained hypocrisy and a more difficult situation for gay clergy to tolerate.

The Eighties – The run-up to Higton

One of the milestones in the recent history of the topic, the 1987 "Higton Debate", is dealt with in the next section. What was the situation during the earlier part of this, the decade in which HIV/AIDS arrived in Britain?

It was in 1981 that AIDS was first recognised in the United States, and a year later that the first death in Britain officially attributed to the disease occurred. This was the death of Terrence Higgins, in memory of whom a trust was formed to provide support for people with HIV/AIDS. At that time, contracting AIDS was always fatal. The average life expectancy of a patient was eighteen months. There was fear and often hysteria amongst the general public, who felt that people with HIV had brought it upon themselves, and, terrified of contracting it, shunned anyone known to be HIV positive, despite the fact that the virus could not be passed on by ordinary contact.

"AIDS is God's judgment" was one of the dominant themes emerging from the interviews with the gay clergymen, some of whom had worked among those who contracted it. Greg recalled headlines referring to the *"AIDS plague...The word 'plague' was a very emotive word in those days"*. He became involved with AIDS patients as a hospital chaplain, and *"set up a support group and a helpline, which was run by the Church. But I became more and more frustrated with the attitude of the Church to the whole HIV/AIDS thing."*

Gareth also recalled this difficult time: *"And then of course AIDS hit very fast into the eighties. A lot of us got involved in working with people who died who were friends of ours, and preparing their funerals. It actually for me as a young priest, it seemed terribly relevant to be a priest. We were doing what felt like very frontline work. You were meeting people, preparing them for death and their funerals, and then burying them, often within a space of six months, or a year, or two years.... With the AIDS crisis, you just saw this kind of resurgence of poor thinking. You know, 'AIDS is God's judgment'. Really crap things were being said and being done. So it was very interesting to be a priest and getting on with the work, and actually engage with trying to bring some level of good news within these situations. And I then found that I was working against the Church as opposed to being part of doing church work."*

Another interviewee who had worked amongst AIDS patients was Graham, who was slightly more positive about the Church's response: *"And when HIV and AIDS came along, I got dragged into that as well. Quite a lot of young men used to just come along and say, 'How about giving me a hand to die?' Because they all had to die."* He went on to tell me that he *"did go and see my bishop, and the other bishops, and said to them, 'What are you going to do? We need to be ready for when the day comes.' Well, it wasn't long before of course there was a priest in the diocese who we knew very well. They did, to their credit, they said they would look at pensions and early retirement, and to see if St Luke's Hospital for the Clergy would take people with HIV. They wouldn't. But they did ask. So they did start to get ready, because of course there were several clergy who had HIV."*

Despite all of this, the interviewees agreed that homosexuality was still not an issue in the Church. Gavin was accepted for ordination at this time and he told me, *"And [my sexuality] certainly wasn't a factor. Because I never spoke of it. And this was in the days when you really didn't, and you wouldn't have been expected to. I mean, I first offered for ordination in the early eighties. And nobody ever asked me about sexuality, as far as I can remember."* In fact, *"I found that I could be myself in the Church, and it was a safe place to be gay. And that seems an extraordinary thing to say, doesn't it. You would never say that now."* Gareth was also selected during this time and he agreed that *"in those days, they weren't so obsessed with it.... They were more concerned that you did the job of a priest by ministering."*

Public awareness of homosexuals within the Church was, however, dawning. George explained: *"I think Outrage and Peter Tatchell, where various bishops and senior clergy were being outed and were seen as being hypocrites by voting for particular practice of lifestyle of celibacy for homosexuals and not wanting to ordain clergy who were homosexual, and yet they themselves were homosexual in orientation. So there was all that in the eighties, which hit the press. So there was a change of culture, I think, in the eighties, and that obviously involved the Church."* Roland described how he had previously been oblivious to any homosexuals who may have been in his congregation, but that it was in the eighties that he became aware of a male couple who lived together and realised that this was the nature of their relationship.

Theological colleges were continuing to accept gay students, the Gloucester Report having failed to give the principals the guidance they sought. Giles said of the students with whom he trained, *"With no exaggeration I would say about 25 of the 35 were gay. Probably about 20 of those quite openly so. But only openly so among their own kind, so they'd be open within the college context and with certain friends discreetly."*

A prominent memory for Roy was of being *"simply staggered"* when he went to a conference about homosexuality during the early eighties for people involved in selecting and training ordinands. *"Now I've never quite known whether that meeting was typical or not. What did emerge was quite clear that some time in the sixties and seventies, certain bishops and certain theological college principals were actually conniving at it.... But what happened was that certain colleges became pretty notorious. I don't mind mentioning that to you because I think it was pretty well known. Places like St Stephen's House where David Hope was appointed principal to sort the mess out - there was so much of that sort of thing going on."*

Asked whether it was the case that theological colleges were taking homosexuals, Graham replied, *"Yes. I think they had to be celibate. I think that was the deal."* He claimed that of the 200 members of the Clergy Consultation, a group set up to support homosexual clergy, only 15 claimed to have a partner. George was keen to stress that he had always been celibate. The consensus among the interviewees, therefore, was that there were many clergy of homosexual orientation in the Church during this time, but there was some divergence of view about how many of them were sexually active. Asked whether Tony Higton was right in thinking there were a lot of gay clergy in the Church when he introduced his motion to Synod in 1987, Graham replied, *"Heavens! Well there were of course. But whether they were promiscuous, as he said everybody was, or whether they were in partnerships..."* What is clear is that, despite the official attitude that homosexuality was sinful and unacceptable in the Church, there was a significant number of bishops and college principals who, whatever their public utterances, were prepared furtively to ordain and appoint homosexuals.

The Higton Debate – a turning point?

Some Issues in Human Sexuality states that the 1987 Synod motion that was passed as a result of the private members' motion brought by the Revd Tony Higton is currently one of the two most authoritative Church of England statements on the issue of homosexuality, the other being *Issues in Human Sexuality*. Since the Church had not accepted the reports on the matter that had been completed during the previous ten years, the passing of the Higton motion was the first occasion when traditional biblical teaching on homosexuality had been officially affirmed and same-sex "genital acts" denounced as falling short of the ideal. Since the motion stated that "all Christians are called to be exemplary in all spheres of morality, and that holiness of life is particularly required of Christian leaders", how did this affect homosexual clergymen? Did the passing of the Higton motion mark a turning point in the way they could conduct their ministries?

It was felt by the interviewees that negative attitudes to homosexuality emerged from the debate. Despite the original motion being about sexual morality in general, Graham felt that

"[Higton] wasn't interested in second marriages, which of course he mentioned, or fornication, or all the other things. He was really having a good bash at gay and lesbian people." Higton told Stephen Bates much later that "My motivation was not to attack the homosexual community but their beliefs" (Bates 2005:116). Nevertheless, Roy, who was present at the debate in 1987, recalled laughingly, *"I remember [Higton] reading off statistic after statistic when he was moving something on anti homosexuality, and David Edwards, who was from the more liberal wing said, 'I do wish he wouldn't gloat quite so much when he reads all the statistics!'"*

Guy spoke incredulously of the terminology, "genital acts", that was used by Higton to refer to same-sex behaviour: *"It was a quite telling and quite interesting thing that nobody stood up to say, 'You can't talk about other human beings like this. Genital Acts? What on earth are they? Is that what you do with your wife? Did you have a nice genital act this morning?' Apart from the fact that it would be a very peculiar thing to talk about at all, it would be a very bizarre way of talking about it."* He also considered that the debate started a near witch hunt for homosexuals in the Church, and also that the passing of the motion did not reflect *"the mind of the Church of England as a whole. Certainly not the mind of the Church of England if it could be made to think about it."*

It seemed to Gavin *"that what that debate was saying was, 'Excuse me, but do we believe in the Bible or don't we?' And people were being forced to stand up and be counted, I think probably for the first time really."* He therefore felt that *"there was a bit of a sea change there."*

Other interviewees also thought that the Higton Debate marked a turning point in replacing the liberal agenda that had been creeping into the Church. This was the opinion of Graham, George and Gus. Roy was appointed to a senior position the year after the Debate and remembers that *"almost the first question was what was my view on homosexuality and what would I do, straight out at the press conference. So by then it was hot potato stuff."*

Gerald described the Higton Debate as *"a watershed"*. He thought that before then, *"you had to be pretty stupid, as a gay priest, not to be able to find senior clergy in the diocese you wanted to live in who would operate on the 'don't ask, don't tell' basis, as long as you were seen to be a good priest. But from that time on, it really has become, you know... And it's an awful shame because I hated seeing that happen, so that gay clergy became much more fearful, and anxious to be seen to be conforming. Also having to get into all sorts of subterfuges to conceal the relationships which they might have. And of course the pressures on them, certainly not to have anyone lodging in the vicarage who might be suspect."*

The Higton Debate therefore tried to put a stop to the furtive ordination of homosexuals. In this, Higton does not seem to have succeeded. Rather, the furtiveness had to increase now that public awareness had been drawn to it. In addition, it created the beginning of the increasing atmosphere of fear in which gay clergy have had to carry out their ministries.

Negative feelings about 'Issues', or "Why not 'Issues in Aardvark Sexuality'?"

Since the Foreword of the 2003 report, *Some Issues in Human Sexuality*, explains that what follows does not seek to change the position of the House of Bishops from the one expressed in *Issues in Human Sexuality*, it may be assumed that the position conveyed in the 1991 report has still not changed. More than twenty years after it was published, candidates for the priesthood still have to agree to abide by the conclusion of *Issues*, specifically that any sexual relationship must only take place within marriage. Same-sex relationships are acceptable in certain circumstances for lay people, but never for clergy.

The feelings of the gay respondents towards this significant report were uniformly negative. Even the title was considered by Guy to be absurd: *"Issues in Human Sexuality? – Oh, can't we talk about aardvarks? I'm sure they've got transgender issues you know,"* he said sarcastically, resonating with a letter published in the Church Times (November 14th 2003) which asked, "Why is it that the titles of church reports speak of human sexuality rather than just sexuality? Are there other committees of bishops producing reports on issues in canine sexuality, bovine sexuality, reptilian sexuality, or even angelic sexuality?"

The words *"appalling"*, *"ridiculous"* and *"nonsense"* were used by Gordon, Guy and Gavin to describe the report. Gordon felt that *"the last bit at the end I think is spiteful"*. Gavin thought that the report *"has come to be used, it seems to me, as a sort of touchstone as to whether somebody is acceptable or not."* Guy was amazed by the terminology used: *"Have you ever heard a normal person use the word 'homophile' to describe gay people?"* It is certainly not a term used commonly in relevant literature and notably it is not used in the later report, *Some Issues in Human Sexuality*, the Foreword of which explains its use of more recognised terminology.

The gay interviewees were scathing of the authority which the Church affords to *Issues*. Gavin pointed out that *"it's only ever been and still only is officially a discussion document. It's talked about as if it were the Church's addition to the Thirty-Nine Articles or something. And it simply isn't."* It was the belief of Gordon that *"bishops really love it, because they realise that it's actually useless."* As paragraph 5.18 prevents clergymen apparently in a close friendship with another man being asked about the nature of the relationship, Gordon felt that it gives bishops the excuse not to ask embarrassing questions. Grant laughingly demonstrated the irony of having to declare one's assent to the report: *"What does it mean to say you assent to Issues in Human Sexuality? I mean, it's a document; it exists. You know, there are various ways of semantically getting round that, aren't there."*

As for its relationship to what had gone before, Gordon felt that *"most people would accept that it's an inadequate expression even of what we thought at the time"*. Guy was bemused that the Gloucester Report had advised bisexuals *"to follow the gay route, because that means you're not going to get to a stage where you can't hack it any longer and you run off with a choirboy and destroy a marriage,"* while *Issues* says that *"because being gay is so very very much worse than being straight, if you are bisexual then you've really got to pull your socks up and be as straight as you possibly can!"* Gavin described the report as *"a bit of a rubber stamp on the Higton debate"* and as such an endorsement of the Church's now declared conservative approach to homosexuality.

The publication of the 1991 report marked a significant rise in the hypocrisy of the hierarchy. The conclusion that stable same-sex relationships were acceptable for the laity but not for the clergy was the first time that different, some might say double, standards had been applied regarding this matter. Furthermore, clergy are reassured that, if "the Church's teaching results for any ordained person in a burden grievous to be borne", the bishops will "always be ready to share in any way we can in the bearing of that burden" (para 5.23). Given their previous statement that clergy may not be in same-sex relationships, this expression of concern is remarkable, since any clergyman confiding in his bishop would necessarily risk his position. Indeed, to repeat Gordon's point, bishops actually do not want clergy to confide in them in this way and are glad to have *Issues'* embargo on enquiring into clergymen's lifestyles as an excuse to turn a blind eye.

The 1998 Lambeth Conference – a turning point?

In the Introduction to *An Acceptable Sacrifice?*, its editors, Duncan Dormor and Jeremy Morris, refer to the "rancorous tone of the debate" that preceded the passing of Resolution I.10, and state that this event was "widely seen as an exercise in turning back the clock" (2007:4-5). They point out that, although resolutions passed at any Lambeth Conference have no legislative force in the Church of England, Resolution I.10 has been afforded great moral force and reference was constantly made to it in the controversy over Jeffrey John's appointment as Bishop of Reading in 2003. Dormor and Morris make the assertion that the situation for homosexual members of the Church of England worsened after the 1998 Lambeth Resolution. Some of the interviewees expressed a similar view.

Greg considered that *"the whole homosexuality thing in the Church was just getting out of hand"* in the late nineties and that the Lambeth Resolution was a reflection of this agitation. Both Guy and Giles referred to the bitter tone of the debate mentioned above, with Guy stating that he had *"heard the most incredible stories about the last Anglican Conference and bishops being bribed with mobile phones and laptops and so on by conservative Americans"*. Giles described the atmosphere at the Conference as being *"fuelled by African bishops, from Nigeria and so on, for whom, quite apart from their religious beliefs, but culturally for Africans, homosexuality simply is an abhorrence"*.

One of the supporters of the subsequent Pastoral Statement, which apologised to homosexual Christians for the negative effects of the Resolution was the Rt Revd Kenneth Stevenson. He later wrote in the Church Times (July 11th 2008), "I voted for Lambeth I.10 on that desultory Wednesday afternoon in 1998, and I have regretted it ever since." Unusually, here was a bishop prepared to admit remorse for feeling obliged to support conservative attitudes to homosexuality. The three interviewees mentioned above considered that Resolution I.10 had been *"quite a turning point"*, restarting the discussion within the Church of England about homosexuality in a negative way and giving rise to a situation in which gay clergy, as Giles put it, *"started to batten down the hatches again, from that time, and either denied their sexuality, or just carried on as though their relationships and so on didn't exist."*

Jeffery John – a turning point?

Five years later, the name of a man previously known only

within certain sections of the Church became synonymous with the furore about homosexuality that was now thrust before the general public. All the gay interviewees had something to say about the appointment of and then withdrawal by Jeffrey John as Bishop of Reading. This was almost unanimously seen as a further turning point that caused yet another return to the closet for homosexual clergy who might have been feeling more confident following the appointment of Rowan Williams as Archbishop of Canterbury the previous year.

Jeffrey John was considered by Gavin and Gareth to have been ideal for the position of Bishop of Reading. Gareth's view was that *"Jeffrey John is an outstandingly good priest, and a very good writer and a man of tremendous integrity. He should have risen to the top, because he's just a very able, competent, prayerful, Gospel inspired priest."* It was this integrity, it was felt, that had led him to be open about his long-standing partnership with a male priest with whom he had trained 27 years previously. The fact it was felt necessary for John to state publicly that the relationship had been celibate for some years was described by Gavin as *"Absolutely disgusting. And even then he wasn't made a bishop."* Gareth agreed: *"I felt that was a disgrace really. And even then the evangelicals wouldn't accept it. I think that's just second-rate. I think that we as a Church have sinned."*

The timing of the appointment was thought to be significant, coming as it did so soon into the archiepiscopate of the liberal Rowan Williams. Grant felt, *"The Church was held down during George Carey's archiepiscopate, and a lot of things were waiting to happen. And they saw with the appointment of Rowan, this was a fresh start. And Richard Harries, who had been pro-gay, thought, 'Ah, this is the time to do it.' And as he himself said, he couldn't have predicted the reaction that there was."*

Gavin felt that Jeffrey John had been made *"rather a pawn"*. Of the new Archbishop he said, *"I think that I would guess that those who proposed him were probably a bit naïve. I have the deepest respect for the Archbishop. I have enormous respect for his wisdom and for his intellect, but I don't think he's a very gifted politician. And I would guess that if it had happened a year or so later, then it wouldn't have happened. Because he would have realised that it was impossible."* In 2006, Alan Rusbridger of The Guardian, having asked Rowan Williams why he had not stood up for his beliefs by maintaining his support for Jeffrey John, described the Archbishop's reaction to his question as "just a flicker of exasperation at being pulled back to what was evidently the most painful episode in his career to date." Williams' answer was that it had "a lot to do… with valuing and nurturing unity. …it really is wrong for an archbishop to be the leader of a party; in a polarised and deeply divided church it's particularly important, I think, not to be someone pursuing an agenda that isn't the agenda of the whole" (Guardian, March 21st 2006). In other words, for the sake of the unity of the Anglican Communion, he was prepared, against his personal beliefs about the issue, to, as journalist Andrew Brown had earlier put it, "sell out the gays" (Church Times, June 4th 2004).

Giles knew as soon as he read of Jeffrey John's appointment that it would cause a furore. He himself had been told by the Prime Minister's appointment secretary a few months previously that, because he was in a same-sex partnership about which he was not prepared to dissemble, in the current climate after the Lambeth 1998 resolution no "significant" appointments were open to him. *"So I said, 'The poor sod! If it gets out, they will crucify him!' And look what happened."*

The Jeffrey John episode was considered to be a turning point by Giles, who thought it *"turned the clock back thirty years"*. Grant, too, had *"got the impression that the Church was rather more open. But now I think that we're in a worse situation because of the evangelical backlash to Jeffrey John."*

Gareth laughed at the idea that Jeffrey John would have been "the first gay bishop", as he was constantly described. He, and others, told me that there were already gay bishops, but that they *"just spend the whole of their ministry hiding"*. Giles portrayed the situation after 2003 thus: *"Not only are these appointments closed to people, to good able people; but also of course a lot of gay clergy have gone back into the closet."*

The hypocrisy of those involved in the fiasco, including, it could be argued, that of John himself in his willingness to collude by making a statement on the nature of his relationship, was thus agreed to have made the situation even more difficult for gay clergymen. Yet still they continued to tolerate it.

The Noughties – Polarisation rules ok.

The title of the paper written in 2003 by sociologists Alasdair Crockett and David Voas following analysis of empirical evidence covering two decades from the British Social Attitudes and British Household Panel surveys is an accurate indicator of the situation during the final decade of this study. *A Divergence of Views: Attitude change and the religious crisis over homosexuality* concludes from the researchers' analysis of responses to questions about attitudes to sexual relationships between homosexuals that there is "a large and growing generation gap, a large and growing gender gap, and most importantly for the churches a large and growing gap between liberal and conservative Christians" (para 2.5).

The contributions of the interviewees supported the conclusion that "divergence of views" or polarisation summarises the noughties. The interviewees, particularly the gay ones, felt that homosexuality was now recognised and widely accepted by society. There was no longer such a fear of AIDS. Greg *"faded out"* of working with HIV/AIDS patients in 2000. He explained why: *"The numbers now in the heterosexual population in the western world are beginning to catch up, if not overtake the gay cases. And because it is now a long-term illness and not a life threatening one, I think people are less cautious and less worried about it."*

Crockett and Voas also noted that attitudes became less tolerant during the eighties, "presumably" because of the "AIDS panic", but that, as worries over AIDS diminished in the nineties, "acceptance of same-sex relationships increased steadily and rapidly" (para 3.3).

Homosexuality became an everyday topic, with gay characters kissing in early evening soap operas, and, as Gareth mentioned, a gay wedding on The Archers. Richard felt that *"Perhaps the biggest change has been greater readiness to engage in dialogue on these issues."* Certainly when I was discussing the forty-year period and subject of my research in the presence of an elderly lady, she commented, "Forty years ago, we wouldn't have been having this conversation."

Gus thought that, in the past, no one concerned themselves with your personal life, *"whereas now I think everybody's asked endlessly about who they are. And you have to take sides now, don't you. I mean, you are either gay or not."* This resonated with an item on an afternoon radio show (Radio 2, October 31st 2007) in which listeners were told that a grandfather had been surprised to be asked to state his sexual orientation on a council survey about garden waste.

For Greg, the advent of civil partnerships during this decade was the greatest turning point in the recent past: *"I think people were getting more vociferous about gay issues. And I think that has moved on a step with civil partnerships, because, from what I can make out, there are quite a few clergy who have gone into civil partnerships, probably to the surprise of the Church as a whole."* Of the twelve gay clergymen that were interviewed, four had already had a civil partnership ceremony and others were considering it with their long-term partner. This is, however, the only way it is possible for a gay clergyman to declare himself, and then, theoretically at least, only if he is prepared to state his relationship to be celibate.

It was believed by the gay interviewees that, in contrast to the acceptance of homosexuality by society, the official Church of

England position was more intolerant than ever. It was thought to be harder to be a gay priest, and in fact Giles, because of *"the Church's particular angst, both currently and certainly in the last ten years, about homosexuality and gay clergy, the Church endlessly getting its knickers in a twist about sexuality and people's private lives"*, had recently decided to become a chaplain, a significantly less high profile position than his previous one. Gavin thought that *"the way the Church has gradually gone since the Higton debate seems to make it less and less likely that there could be an openly gay bishop."*

All bishops now have to toe the party line, rather than following their own beliefs, asserted Guy ruefully: *"And so they can say, 'Well I used to believe that before I was a bishop, but now I have to...' Well, hang on; why were you made a bishop if it wasn't because of what you believe?"* And Gavin felt that *"The evangelicals seem to hold all the cards today."*

Giles, who felt he had himself suffered from discrimination, was outraged that, while the Equality Act (Sexual Orientation) Regulations made discrimination against homosexuals illegal, religious organisations were exempt from this. He summed up the hypocrisy of this: *"I don't see any difference between saying to somebody, 'I'm sorry. We think you're fabulous, but you're black and you can't have that job,' to saying, 'I'm sorry. We think you're fabulous, but you're gay and you can't have that job.' In my mind they are two sides of the same coin. But the Church does it. The Church gets away with it. And what I find quite extraordinary is that the Church, which ought to be the organisation which champions human rights, and human equality and everything else, the good old Church of England was the one organisation which, through its bishops in the House of Lords, managed to get an exemption from the Government in relation to its employments issues vis-à-vis the recent human rights legislation. The bishops of the Church of England in the House of Lords got an exemption from human rights legislation, in order – why? – in order that they could continue to discriminate against their clergy and who they employ in their churches. And the Government gave them that exemption. Now that seems to me to be intolerable! Quite extraordinary!"*

It was generally felt that the Church's perceived obsession with sex was, in Giles's words, *"hampering its mission, and undermining its credibility, in a society which is increasingly more tolerant".* Gareth described the situation thus: *"I think the Church is struggling to find a way ahead with decreased numbers, decreased money, decreased interest within society, and the Church has latched on to this, which is probably the most irrelevant of issues for most people, who are trying to go on a spiritual journey."* The impact of the media was seen by some interviewees to be fuelling this state of affairs, with Gareth's view being that the press' intention was to present *"a very naïve, happy clappy kind of religion, which can then easily be rejected".* Various other issues were mentioned as being far worthier of the Church's attention and yet seeming to be classed as less pressing. Grant said of the Church, *"You know, it's obsessed with it [sex], and much less is said about global issues or huge international financial problems, or what have you."*

Desmond Tutu was mentioned by two interviewees as being concerned about this. Gus quoted a radio interview with Tutu he had recently heard: *"Archbishop Tutu was saying how saddened he was that the Church was spending all its time on homophobia, instead of seeing to all the troubles and difficulties and sadnesses in the world. And I remember, he said these words: 'If God is homophobic, I wouldn't be able to worship that God'. Wonderful words, weren't they?"* Tutu wrote the Foreword to the book, *An Acceptable Sacrifice?,* in which he states, "The answer is simple: No. It is not acceptable for us to discriminate against our brothers and sisters on the basis of sexual orientation just as it was not acceptable for discrimination to exist on the basis of skin colour under Apartheid" (2007:ix). I attended the launch of this book and it was notable that one of the contributors could not be present because he was in Eritrea working with people affected by

HIV/AIDS. Obviously his priorities lay with other issues than homosexuality.

The noughties saw the enthronement of Rowan Williams as Archbishop of Canterbury, and the interviewees viewed this as significant in bringing about the situation regarding homosexuality during this decade. Richard summed up the changes brought about thus: *"I think that Archbishop George Carey did all that he could to stifle discussion on this subject. He came from the evangelical tradition, and was not prepared to countenance any change in the Church's stance. His retirement opened the floodgates, and the liberal attitude of Archbishop Rowan Williams gave the green light for a great deal of discussion and changing of attitudes."*

Graham agreed with this assessment of the two Archbishops. He told me that, during Carey's archiepiscopacy, Williams *"was very pro-gay, and came with me to see Archbishop Carey. There were six of us. We went to lunch, and we tried to explain to him that the Church has now got to move forward and accept gay and lesbian people. And Rowan came and was a very good theological resource. Carey didn't take any notice of course."*

It was because of Rowan Williams' liberal views about homosexuality that there was so much opposition to his appointment in 2002. Guy believed that those who appointed Rowan Williams as Archbishop of Canterbury did so because he was *"somebody who had those liberal views, albeit from the perspective of a personal belief of a deeply orthodox person in terms of his religiosity and his spirituality"*. Moreover, he felt that they *"appointed him young, in order to see through this question. He could have had twenty years as Archbishop of Canterbury, poor bloke. In which case it could be that he was appointed to sort these things out in these twenty years. And instead it's all blown up straightaway."* It was, of course, only the next year that the announcement of Jeffrey John's appointment and the subsequent furore put the liberal views of the new Archbishop to the test.

When looking back at the events of 2003 Richard Harries

stated, "I'm not critical of the role of the archbishop, because I understand very well the pressures on him and his deep desire to hold the Anglican Communion together" (Peart-Binns 2007:214). Guy's perception was less sympathetic. What the liberals had failed to appreciate, he said, was that Rowan Williams himself thought that *"he was appointed as someone to shape himself to the office instead of a person who could shape the office by his personality"*.

And what of the future? Some of the interviewees were pessimistic about the prospects for the Church of England. Giles said, *"You know, I really do think, if I'm honest with you, that we're now in the dying days of the Church of England. I do. I think there is such massive disintegration going on in every area of its life; I don't think it can survive."*

The perceived stalemate in the Church of England was thought to be exacerbated by the perceived stalemate in the Anglican Communion, which was considered by Gordon to have a *"post-imperialist"* element. He explained, *"I do think there's an element of 'You came over here. You took our countries. You took our gold. And you told us how to behave. And now you're not behaving and we will make you behave.' I think at some emotional level, that is what's going on. Which has got nothing to do with the Gospel, any more than the original conquest of those countries had, and possibly even the imposition of the Gospel."*

Grant wondered, *"And if the Communion splits, what will that mean for the Church of England? People withholding parish shares."* This prediction resonated with the threat by some evangelical parishes of withholding their parish shares if the consecration of Jeffrey John went ahead. "We were also concerned that money given sacrificially by members of the congregation should not be used to subsidise ministry that has departed from the teaching of scripture," explained a churchwarden of an Oxford church looking back to 2003, (Letters, Church Times, April 28th 2006).

In his book about "The End of the Church of England",

Michael Hampson bemoans the part evangelical financial strength played in preventing Jeffrey John's preferment. He asserts that a precedent has been set: "the bishop now does what the fundamentalists say, or the whole diocesan edifice will come crashing down" (2006:176). This was the supreme act of hypocrisy of the noughties. Jeffrey John's appointment was withdrawn by those who had approved it, because they were afraid of the power of the evangelicals. The situation for gay clergymen was made yet more difficult, ironically partly because of society's increasing awareness of homosexuals. Yet even Jeffrey John himself continued to tolerate it.

CHAPTER 4

THE OXYMORON OF GAY PRIESTS

All clergy and prospective ordinands must assent to the conclusion of the 1991 report, *Issues in Human Sexuality*, as a way of compelling them to agree not to engage in physically expressed same-sex relationships. It follows therefore that theoretically there are no practising homosexual priests. As far as the Church of England is concerned, a gay priest is an oxymoron, a contradiction in terms. However, the fact that a significant number of practising homosexual priests have been identified, not only for the present study but also by previous researchers (see, for example, Yip 1999 and Keenan 2008, 2009), demonstrates that in fact there is an indeterminate but evidently considerable number in various forms of ministry.

By examining the contributions from the interviewees, this chapter explores the concept of this oxymoron and the hypocrisy involved in maintaining it.

The ironies of Issues' conclusion, or "The whole thing is messy"

The contributions from the gay interviewees about the conclusion of *Issues in Human Sexuality* gave insights into how those clergy who are fundamentally affected by it viewed the distinction it makes between clergy and laity.

Gordon's assessment of the distinction was: *"It says, 'We have concluded that you probably won't burn as a Christian. But you will do as a clergyman.' And that seems to me to have nothing to do with sexuality and more to do with your theology of priesthood. That's what it's about. It's about publicly representing them. I mean they don't mind what you do with your life, but they don't want you saying that you're doing it on their behalf."* George was more sympathetic to the Church's position in the way he viewed the conclusion: "*I think what is significant about the ordained person is that you are very much in public life. It goes without question that there is a kind of lifestyle that is required of all Christian people, but there is a specific kind of lifestyle, in my view, expected of the ordained person.*" However, even he felt that, with regard to the distinction made between lay and ordained people, "*the whole thing is messy. There's no consistency*". So, does the conclusion of *Issues* represent double standards in the Church's approach?

The idea that clergy were in some sense fundamentally different and superior was rejected by Giles: "*I don't see this huge difference, in the way that Issues in Human Sexuality did, between clergy and lay people. Some people see the clergy as being set apart and practically being a different species. As far as I'm concerned, as someone said to me years ago and I've never forgotten it, he said in his experience the best priests are those who have forgotten that they're priests. On another occasion he said to me, 'At the end of the day, I don't think God gives two hoots whether you're a priest, a dustman, a teacher or what you are. What He does hope for is that we'll be faithful.'*"

Greg agreed: "*Yes, this is where the Church is applying a double standard. If we're talking about setting an example, Christians as a whole as the Body of Christ should be setting the same example. To say it's ok for laity but not ok for clergy is elevating the clergy to a plain they don't really deserve to be on, and I think it's saying fairly derogatory things about the laity – that they're second class in comparison!*" Grant, too, thought, "*Either it's ok or it's not ok. That puts clergy on more of a pedestal than they should be anyway when it comes to the whole people of God. Being ordained is only one way of being a baptised Christian.*"

While being in a same-sex partnership as an ordinary lay member of the Church is deemed acceptable by *Issues*, it is not clear whether holding any sort of lay office is permissible. Greg told me that it was the incumbent's decision as far as minor roles were concerned, while more high profile offices were the subject of election by the PCC or those on the electoral roll. The bishop would probably not be aware of the sexuality of the majority of lay officers, despite being required to authorise some of them. George, who was in a senior position, explained that *"the Church is sitting in a world where a significant number of homosexual people attend those churches, and there are some people in authority, church-wardens if you like, who are of homosexual orientation and live with their partners. Some have had civil partnerships. I'm aware of that. I accept it. It's not for me to interfere."* However, in July 2006, John Reaney was turned down as a lay youth worker in the diocese of Hereford because he was openly homosexual, despite pledging to remain celibate for the duration of the post.

The irony of the distinction made by *Issues* was summed up by Grant in recalling that *"there was a joke when I was at theological college: What do you do then if your partner is a layperson and you're a priest? Is it all right if you just lie back and don't do anything yourself?"*

Attitudes to lay authority for homosexuals, or "People of good conscience"

The retired respondents, who were of a generation more likely to be disapproving of homosexuals according to Crockett and Voas' study (2003), were generally happy for them to hold lay office with provisos. They agreed with Greg that lay involvement was at the incumbent's discretion. None were aware that there had ever been any episcopal directives on the matter, and Roy, a senior clergyman, felt, *"I've taken it generally that the laity are outside the bishop's concern anyway. ... But I mean if you've got two lay people in a church who are living together, it's not going to come to the bishop's ears for a moment. He has no power if it did come to his ears. I suppose the only way it would come of course is if the clergyman refused them communion, on the grounds they were openly notorious evil livers, then a decision would have to be made I suppose."*

There were some minor reservations about lay office, the

strongest coming from Reginald, the oldest of the respondents. It was, however, generally felt that lay authority was possible for gay people thought to be of good standing and conscience. Roland defined this by explaining that *"the Church recognises that people may do something which is objectively wrong, but do it in good conscience."* Richard agreed: *"Although nobody ever mentioned the subject, I am quite sure that we did have homosexuals serving at the altar and on the PCC. If I was in the same position again, I would take the same line, because I would accept that such people were true to their own consciences, even though the Church could not officially condone any homosexual activities."*

Ralph's view was that *"obviously [the incumbent] must have full knowledge of the person and their background, and that sort of thing. You don't – at least I hope you don't – appoint to positions like that lightly anyway. It's not just about whether the person is a homosexual, but whether they have the background and responsibility to take on such a position."* And Robin said, *"I would simply say that I would play it by ear, and trust my judgment of people as far as I can."*

Two other themes making up this dimension were provisos. One was that lay authority for homosexuals was all right if no one talked about the fact: *"What happens behind closed doors is people's own business,"* said RR1, resonating with the practice of turning a blind eye which it will be contended is the prevailing attitude of the Church to homosexuals. The second was that it was important that the congregation did not mind. *"Something must be added, I think, about how other people regard it"*, said Roy. *"And every parish priest when appointing somebody to such a sensitive position, would have to be aware of the feelings in the PCC and the congregation"*, said Ralph. Robert agreed: *"You certainly wouldn't do it if the majority of the congregation found it to be offensive."*

As a lay person, then, it is possible not only to find acceptance for oneself and one's partner in the Church, but also to be appointed to lay office. Clearly homosexual lay people need to choose carefully which church they attend. An evangelical church would be most unlikely to welcome them and would almost certainly not consider them suitable for lay office. However, churches do exist, mainly in towns and cities, in which lay homosexuals feel comfortable and valued. Although the practice of welcoming everyone would seem to be one to which the Church in general should aspire, gay people need to seek churches with a policy of inclusiveness, which, due to the prevailing nervousness about being seen to approve of homosexuals, may not always be explicitly stated.

Priestly changes, or "A strange idea to start with"

But what of clergy? The conclusion of *Issues* leaves no doubt that, while committed gay relationships among lay people are tolerable, to be a priest in a same-sex relationship is not permissible. Regardless of the double standards this represents, such discrimination is at odds with the changed attitudes to gay people within society. The retired clergymen remarked on several significant changes in priestly circumstances that had taken place since their own ordinations more than forty years ago. There are two that are noteworthy here as examples of how the Church altered its policies during the forty-year period to fall in line with changed secular practice and attitudes.

As far as the onlooker is concerned, the most obvious change is the fact that in 1967 it was impossible for a woman to be ordained as a priest. The passing of the measure by the General Synod in November 1993 to permit the ordination of women made a huge difference to the structure of the priesthood, with a significant percentage of Church of England clergy now being female. For a long time, opposition to women's ordination to the priesthood from both the Anglo-Catholic and evangelical wings prevented this from being passed. As with homosexuality, the objection from the evangelical wing was based on the grounds that such a measure was contrary to scripture. What changed their thinking to the extent necessary for the two-thirds majority in 1992 was largely a change in their interpretation of the relevant biblical passages.

The retired respondents' generation had seen the role of a woman develop from predominantly being someone who stayed at home to care for her family to being an equal to a man in almost every sphere of the workplace. Since, as with homosexuality, the Church was the only place where a woman did not have equality of opportunity, it was thought right to redress this in 1992. Reginald's view of this change was probably typical of those who witnessed it: "*It was a strange idea to start with. But one accepted it I think. Because the situation has changed. Women are different now than what they were.*" Homosexuals, too, are considered differently now. Might it not be that those for whom an openly gay clergyman might seem "a strange idea to start with" would come to accept this in the same way?

Roy brought up the other significant area in which the Church has changed its policy on who is a suitable person to be ordained: "*And in fact another thing that has changed, is of course the attitude to divorce. At one time it would be unthinkable - if a clergyman was divorced, very often he was made to leave the ministry*". *Some Issues* tells us that this was a matter in which the Church "sought to combine long-held principles with a response to changes in society in a mature and responsible pastoral manner" (para 1.5.2). The growth of divorce began in the mid-sixties, and the next twenty years saw numbers of divorcing couples steadily increase. Accordingly the General Synod gradually accepted the principle that remarriage of divorced people should be permitted. A service of blessing after a civil marriage of divorced people was approved by the House of Bishops, and it was in 1990 that people who had remarried during the lifetime of a former partner, or who were married to someone who had done so, were permitted to be considered for ordination.

Thus the Church has seen fit to allow women and divorcees to be ordained in order to be in line with new social attitudes. It has not, however, seen fit to do the same for homosexuals.

Another change to priestly circumstances worth noting here was outlined by Roy: *"Everybody had the freehold at one time. It really means that no one can really touch you unless you do something really bad."* Roger explained further: *"A parson's freehold made him independent in the community and no one could say him nay, not unless he did something against the law. All you were obliged to do was to say the office and visit anyone who asked you to. Nowadays you tend to be given the post of 'priest-in-charge', the implication being that you can be removed if you are not satisfactory."* The significance of this for the homosexual is that, when he had the freehold, after the decriminalisation in 1967 it would be unlikely that he could be removed from his post on the grounds of his sexuality. Now that he is almost certainly "priest-in-charge", he necessarily lives under the fear that he can be dismissed if objections arising from his sexuality are raised.

Gay clergy: not allowed, but lots anyway

Despite the prohibition on practising homosexuals being part of the ordained clergy of the Church of England, it proved possible, without much difficulty, to find eleven to interview. (The twelfth maintained that he had never been sexually active.) Moreover, it was clear that these constituted only a small proportion of the homosexual population of ordained clergy. Greg estimated, *"You know, they talk about 5% of the population being gay, and 10% of the clergy. I'd want to up that figure to nearer 15 or 20%."* Grant's estimate was similar: *"I don't know what the proportion is, but if you say one in ten in society, there must be more among the clergy really."* In 1990, Dr Ben Fletcher estimated that around 15% of Church of England clergy were homosexual. In his study about stress amongst clergy, he felt that it was clear from his estimates that homosexuals formed "a very significant proportion of Church of England clergy, and should be considered an important section" (1990:65).

These figures are supported by the fact that some of the gay respondents told me that other students who trained with them at theological college were homosexual. George said there was a *"significant number"*, Greg estimated that 30% of the students at his college were gay, while Grant declared, *"I went to a college where I suppose 80% of the students must have been gay."*

The responses about gay clergy suggested that they could be found at every level. Greg laughingly told me that in one of his appointments, *"Most of the staff were gay! The team rector, two team vicars. But there was nothing untoward in that."* As well as existing amongst the ordinary clergy, there was suggestion that homosexuals could be found in the episcopacy: *"What saddens me that the focus is all on the clergy, and yet the House of Bishops has gays in its midst,"* intimated Greg. I asked if he thought these bishops were sexually active and he replied, *"Well, that I wouldn't go as far as to say."* This was supported by George, who told me, *"And indeed we have some ordaining bishops today who are of a homosexual orientation."*

George included other senior clergy in the groups which he knew to contain homosexuals. Two of the interviewees came within this category. He also said that, *"Some who are married have a homosexual orientation, I'd suggest."* Greg agreed that *"There are a lot of clergy who are gay and married."* Graham was one of the respondents who spoke about the confidential support organisation, Clergy Consultation. Founded in 1976, its website explains that it "provides mutual support and advice, offers a forum for education and discussion, and responds to the professional and pastoral needs of homosexual clergy." Speaking of his involvement some years ago, Graham told me, *"The most difficult of all were the married gay clergy."* How sad that, such is the stigma attached to being homosexual in the Church, some have felt it expedient to enter a covenant which must necessarily be unfulfilling for both partners.

The location of all these homosexual clergy would appear to

be largely in London. Graham recounted that it is much easier to be a homosexual clergyman in London. Southwark diocese, he maintained, *"is stuffed full of gay clergy"*. One of the interviewees who worked in London described himself as being *"in a fortunate position. I'm in an area in which in the adjacent six parishes, four of us are gay men, as priests. I think if you're in an urban area, you are likely to have that more than if you're in a rural area."* Gordon gave a reason for the prevalence in the capital: *"In some deaneries in central London, it's exclusive, because nobody else would live there. You'd never get somebody with a family to move to these places."*

Leo was an ordinand at the time of his interview. In the short time since then, he has not only been ordained in London, but has obtained a minor, but significant, preferment there. He recounted, *"As I got into the discernment process itself and had interviews with people, I'd already agreed with my rector that the principle of the diocese, 'Ask no questions, tell no lies,' was something to work with really, because that was the way in which they would maximise the quality of priests that they would get. And especially in the big city, where there are lots of parishes where priests with family, or just married, couldn't see themselves going. So it became clear early on that there was a game to be played."*

In urban areas, the "game" suits all the players for the reasons stated above. Speaking of a friend in rural ministry, however, Grant said, *"I don't know how they manage to do it. I think it's terribly easy to find yourself living your life with insufficient support mechanisms."* Graham agreed that rural clergy *"have the most difficult time of all."* One of the interviewees who was himself the incumbent of village parishes thought that *"it was actually quite a brave step to come into rural ministry, with a partner in tow. I didn't think about it at the time. I just felt it was something I wanted to come and do."*

Gay clergy: not allowed, so how do they cope?

As a result of the developments in attitudes to homosexuality both by the Church and by society since 1967, the homosexual interviewees expressed the feeling that it was increasingly difficult to live out their calling as a gay clergyman. Gerald described how he had seen over the years *"paradoxically, as secular society has become more and more open, and the whole issue of sexuality following the Wolfenden initiative, it's become more difficult for clergy, because attitudes, as we all know, have hardened over what is required of clergy, particularly since the 1980s, when there was that development in the Synod in '87."* Geoff agreed that *"We had become used to living with what were seen as creative tensions, but polarisation has made them more than this."*

How, then, did the gay clergy cope with their increasingly difficult position? Various strategies were outlined, and they were grouped into the other themes that made up this dimension. The first theme was "By being discreet". Giles explained that one way of doing this was to *"go along with the story of, oh you know, 'Just waiting for the right girl to come along' and that sort of thing. As indeed I did myself, to a certain extent, because of course there's the question of sensitivity. Obviously if you're a single priest, then people are going to say, 'When are you going to meet the right girl and settle down?' For me it would be quite improper and quite inappropriate then to say, 'Well actually, I happen to be gay. It's just not going to happen. In fact I'm waiting for the right boy to come along.'"*

Greg felt that gay relationships were acceptable to people now if they were discreet, as he felt his was. And for Gareth, being discreet meant that it was not that his activities were *"secret, but they are private, and if I'm to do anything as a priest, it's to present Christ, which isn't about presenting myself."* However, Gerald felt that many clergy *"regret the extent to which they've had to modify the sort of people they are for public consumption."*

The second theme of how to cope was "By watching your back". Greg had been visited by a neighbouring minister who wanted to know whether rumours that he was in a homosexual relationship were true. He managed to avoid giving a direct answer: *"With hindsight, I would like to have had the courage to say, 'Yes, it's true', but that would have affected so many people in a negative way."* Grant mentioned senior clergymen who have spoken publicly in favour of homosexuals, but recognised that *"people like Colin Slee* (then the Dean of Southwark) *and John Gladwin* (then the Bishop of Chelmsford) *can say those sorts of things publicly. They've got nothing to lose because they're married. They're not going to have their personal lives dragged through the mud. I'm always very glad that there are people who will do that. Whereas if you say, 'I'm a gay priest and this is my partner,' it's very different."* However, he was troubled that by not speaking up when he heard people making anti-gay statements he was *"colluding with them with my silence"*.

Gareth said that, whereas some homosexual clergy are naturally discreet, others feel the need to be so because *"they are quite frightened"*. George agreed that it was necessary for homosexual clergy in a relationship to *"live very discreetly, and fear, possibly, and fear."* Geoff put this more strongly: *"The crying shame is the sense in which we are paralysed in terms of fearfulness."*

As has already been shown, "By working in urban areas" was another strategy and thus the third theme. Grant told me, *"I think the thing about working in a town is that it's more easy to be anonymous in a town, isn't it. I think if you have a vicarage or rectory in a village, it's usually in a very obvious position, and everybody sees who's coming to your driveway, and who is at your house. The whole culture and diversity in towns makes it a lot easier to be a gay priest."*

"By joining support groups" was a popular strategy, and the fourth theme. For Grant, this was achieved by socialising with other homosexual clergymen: *"I've moved in areas where there's been quite a large gay sub-culture, and there's strength in numbers."* For several of the other gay interviewees, Clergy Consultation had proved to be a useful means of support. There are further organisations whose purpose is to help gay Christians, arguably the most high profile being the Lesbian and Gay Christian

Movement. Gareth's view of this was that it *"has done an extremely important job, because I think the Church has failed to do stuff."* None of the interviewees mentioned being a member of this, however, perhaps because, unlike Clergy Consultation, its membership does not offer the confidentiality sadly so essential for clergymen.

It is less usual now for clergy to have the freehold of their parish, but "By having the freehold" was the fifth theme that emerged. Greg had the freehold of his parish and felt that, *"It gives me a degree of security. Personal security. And I feel that if I don't step out of line, then there's nothing anybody can do to ship me out."* Graham agreed that having the freehold *"has been the great saviour of a lot of gay men, and women, that they can't be thrown out without a tremendous fuss."*

The sixth theme was that a good way of coping with being a gay clergyman was "By being in chaplaincies". Gerald explained that *"many gay clergy have found a relief and much more sensible to be in chaplaincies rather than in a parish ministry... It wasn't just the nosy-parkerness of parishes; it's also the power issue again. That you're not in the power of the Church as your employer."* Two of the interviewees worked as hospital chaplains, one as a school chaplain, and another as a prison chaplain, all employed by organisations which, unlike the Church, are Equal Opportunities employers. One of the hospital chaplains recounted that the local bishop was aware that he had had a civil partnership: *"I mean, my line actually was that it was none of his business. You know, seriously. That if he didn't like it, he could lump it. He's not my employer."* The school chaplain made a similar comment: *"I'm not paid by the Church. So they can't control me, which is what they do to other people."*

The final theme that makes up this dimension, "By getting on with the job", indicates that homosexual clergymen are not constantly preoccupied with hiding their sexuality. It was Gareth who said, *"Actually a huge number of clergy just get on with the job."* Most of the gay interviewees expressed the feeling that they were doing this to the best of their ability. Gordon's view of his ministry was, *"I would simply stand by my record. I haven't fiddled with choirboys, and I have done my best to serve the people here as I said that I would."* Greg's approach was similar: *"I do the job the best I can, to the best of my ability, and generally get a positive response, particularly with the occasional offices – baptism, marriage and funerals – which I think are hugely important. I've kept a whole drawer full of thank you letters. I keep those in case I'm ever outed and end up in ecclesiastical courts. If something goes wrong, at least I've got proof that people have appreciated what I've done."*

While Giles was carrying out a parish ministry, *"one didn't go around talking about it [his sexuality] the whole time. It was just part of life."* Gus, referring to typical advice given by a bishop he had known about how to approach one's sexuality, said, *"I think there are some wonderful homosexual priests, aren't there, but they do like the bishop said, 'Don't broadcast it'."* Greg pointed out, *"And you know, gay clergy who have died, you often see in their obituaries the amount they have contributed to the life of the Church."* When civil partnerships began, the Bishop of St Edmundsbury and Ipswich, the Rt. Revd. Richard Lewis, was quoted as saying that gay clergymen "are amongst the best we have, and I am daily thankful for them" (Church Times, November 30th 2005).

However, it is important to stress that it was not suggested that all homosexuals are indiscriminately suitable for the priesthood, nor is that in any way a contention of this book. Grant was at pains to point out that higher standards of moral behaviour should be expected from the clergy, and *"even within sexuality there's a huge distinction, isn't there, between being in a permanent relationship with somebody and leading a promiscuous life."*

"Always at the mercy of bishops" – Episcopal attitudes
It was Guy who summed up the general feeling about the people who have the most influence over ordination and incumbencies:

"You're always at the mercy of bishops... You can say one thing to one bishop and that's fine, and then it can go down the file and then the next bishop reads it who is not favourable, well then there's chaos."

The hypocrisy shown by bishops was made very clear by the themes that emerged in this dimension. The first theme was that "Bishops differ widely in approach", despite the conclusion of *Issues*, which all are supposed to observe. *"The Church is individuals,"* pointed out Gordon, explaining why some bishops are supportive while others are not. Some bishops will not ordain a practising homosexual or license one to a parish, such as the bishop of Gareth's diocese, but, as George noted, *"There are some bishops who don't necessarily follow their own guidelines in this matter."*

The second theme was that "Bishops can privately be kind and supportive", and the gay subjects offered plenty of evidence of this being the case. When Gareth was being interviewed for a position, the bishop asked him if he had someone with whom to go on holiday, adding *"I don't really want to know, but it's important that clergy have people or friends or somebody special that they can go away with."* This bishop was evidently concerned that Gareth should have a happy private life, as were the bishops of Guy and Grant, both of whom reported that their bishops had expressed sympathy on learning that they had separated from their partners.

Gavin's bishop *"is quite a good friend of ours, and knows us both, and that we live together and has been to have dinner with us."* When Gordon spoke about AIDS in a sermon, a lady reported him to his bishop for preaching immorality. The bishop supported Gordon, ringing him to say, *"'I shall offer the lady the chance to come and see me. But I'm writing to her to say that sometimes our minds play tricks on us, and actually I've read your sermon and I agree with every word of it.'"* Graham spoke of one bishop he had who disapproved of homosexuality as unbiblical, but was nevertheless *"warm"* and *"a great supporter"*.

However, evidence was also offered for the third theme, "Bishops' support can be transitory". Guy likened bishops to chameleons, saying one thing in private and another in public. Graham spoke of a bishop who had been to supper with him and his partner, but had not supported him when his sexuality was the underlying cause of some legal difficulties. Giles was contemptuous of this sort of inconsistent support: "*It is hypocrisy, if you're a bishop, and you come and sit at a dining table with you and your partner and have a wonderful meal and drink your wine, and say, 'Oh I think you're so good together', and then the next week to be giving some sort of debate in the House of Lords or speaking to a newspaper and saying, 'Oh I wouldn't ordain a practising homosexual'. It's hypocrisy. It goes on all the time. Of course it does.*"

The night before Gordon was ordained, he went, as is customary, to see the bishop, who apparently said, "'*I want you to know that I wish you well and I will pray for you. But if it goes wrong, you can't come to me looking for help.*'" This resonated with Gareth's opinion that "*They support you until they find out that there's some public kind of thing, or somebody else finds out.*" Bishops presumably feel they have to demonstrate that they are working within the Church's position on the issue, and it could be argued that their desire not to show any kind of public support for gay clergy is therefore understandable. However, they have the collective power to vary the Church's approach, and it is unsurprising that the interviewees found their transitory support hypocritical.

The fourth theme that emerged from the interviews was that "Bishops turn a blind eye unless their hand is forced". This comment from Grant outlines a reason for this: "*The archdeacon here was saying that if you got rid of all the gay clergy, there wouldn't be any priests in this area because people don't want to bring their families up here. Gay clergy tend to work where other people won't go. And the bishops do realise that.*" Grant also suggested another reason for their blind eye: the rules are so widely infringed on many points, such as same-sex blessings, that they are *"beyond discipline"*.

Geoff explained further: *"Most bishops don't want to expend a great deal of energy investigating something that isn't going to build up the Church. An investigation will cause scandal and will not achieve anything positive. Most bishops don't want to go down that route unless a person has behaved in a flagrant way."*

George agreed that bishops would not normally conduct an investigation into the sexuality of a priest unless there was a formal complaint, but that *"I think the exception would be that if they were aware that a clergyperson was leading a particular kind of lifestyle that was affecting his work and if he was seen to be frequenting gay bars and clubs on a regular basis, or there was evidence that he was being promiscuous and having several partners in the course of a week. I mean that would be a very serious matter."* This of course would also be the case if the clergyman was being heterosexually promiscuous.

Gordon believed that the Church position on homosexuality was generally looked on as a formality, but that *"it wouldn't be a formality if they had other reasons to want to wheel you in."* This was born out by Guy's report of being called to see his bishop: *"He was reading through various accusations and then he asked me - which you're not supposed to do on the don't ask, don't tell regime - if I had a significant other, male or female. Of course I should have just told him to get lost... And it was quite clear that, when I said I had a male partner, that finished it."* Without knowing the circumstances of the accusations, it would be inappropriate to surmise about the justice of the dismissal. However, what is clear is that Guy's refusal to collude with the Church's approach ultimately lost him his position.

Partners and lodgers – "Is that "lodger" with a small l or a big L?"

From his experience of working with young gay clergy, Jeffrey

John writes,

> "Almost all of them rejected promiscuity, and feared the futile
> prospect of a series of abortive relationships leading to a
> lonely old age. What they wanted was, precisely, the ideal: the
> hope, like their heterosexual friends, of finding someone to
> love and be wholly given to, someone to grow together with,
> someone who would still be there at the end of the day and at
> the end of their life. That is not a heterosexual hope or a
> homosexual hope; it is a fundamental human hope." (2000:5-
> 6)

The experience of the homosexual interviewees was that it was
precisely achieving the fulfilment of this hope that led to
problems as a gay clergyman. As long as the Church did not
officially know of their relationships, it was content to turn a
blind eye to them. However, when a gay clergyman wanted to be
honest about having a stable partner, it caused trouble. If his
partner lived with him, it was important for his position as a
priest that he should be seen as the "lodger".

*"What I always realised when I was exploring my vocation, was
that, I think I always knew that it was all right as long as I didn't have
a relationship. Or as long as I didn't really have a relationship,"* said
Gavin. He elaborated: *"Yes, you could have a little bit, well, a little
bit of naughtiness here and there, you know. But as soon as it became
anything like a relationship, so that you would have to be open about it,
have to tell people about it, have to be seen out regularly, then that's
quite a different order isn't it?"*

Grant pointed out that, in his tradition, promiscuity could be
dealt with in confession as another lapse: *"But actually the minute
you admit that there's somebody in your life, that makes the situation
worse."* Graham said that he *"was given advice fairly early on that,
if I admitted I had a partner, it would be reasonable for the bishop to
say, 'You've got to go'".* He continued, *"You couldn't really live with*

somebody. *You might have a friend who you went on holiday with, or saw once a week, or that sort of thing you know. But it wasn't a live-in partner."* In other words, the Church discourages the establishment of committed relationships, and certainly deters honesty about those that are established.

When Gordon was pursuing ordination, he *"always assumed, like a lot of people that I knew, that I would get ordained and run a parish and that my partner would be my 'lodger'".* Giles told me that he knew *"lots of clergy who have to play this game... I won't, but I could give you a list of probably about thirty clergy, friends of mine, who all live with their partner, - and when people come to the house, such as you coming today, the partner goes upstairs, and hides away, and stays there until the company's gone, and when the company's gone, he comes down again. If he is spotted on the way to the kitchen or going out of the front door, he's always the lodger."* Bishops are apparently happy to "play this game", since it is shown in other dimensions that they are often unofficially aware of the nature of the relationship.

In inner-city parishes, however, Gavin asserted that the situation was different: *"I don't think you'd have to look too far before you found clergy who were living with their partners quite openly."* One of the interviewees has subsequently been appointed to an inner-city parish with the knowledge and approval of the bishop and churchwardens that he was sharing the vicarage with his partner. Typically, this bishop was prepared to ignore the official prohibition in order to fill this position with someone with suitable gifts.

Grant thought that the attitude of many parishioners whose priest lived with his partner, whether in London or elsewhere was *"'Isn't it nice that Father's got someone staying with him at the vicarage?'"* and that they naturally saw the partner as the priest's lodger. *"You know, you'd say, 'Is that 'lodger' with a small l or a big L?"* The Church's discouragement of gay clergy from honestly professing the kind of stable relationship that heterosexual clergy are encouraged in is clearly lost on such parishioners.

Chances of preferment, or "It would be a hopeless case."

It is generally agreed that the debate about homosexuality became more intense when two openly gay men, Jeffrey John (who subsequently withdrew) and Gene Robinson, were appointed as bishops within the Anglican Communion in 2003. The homosexual interviewees felt that since then their chances of preferment to significant positions in the Church of England had considerably lessened.

"Ambition kills the spirit," thought Gareth, who indicated that he believed ambitious clergy obtained preferment by not revealing their sexuality. *"I never have had any ambitions like that,"* said Gavin, who agreed that ambition thwarts openness and openness thwarts ambition, *"and I think that, if I did, it would be sad for me because it would be a hopeless case."*

Giles had been told when he was summoned to discuss possible preferment that *"'It's not that you're gay. But it's that you have a relationship... I have a number of young, able, gifted, experienced clergy on my books at the moment. I have a larger number of significant jobs which need those young, gifted, energised people. And I can't place them. And the reason I can't place them is because they are in gay relationships, and I can't do it.'"* If Giles had been prepared to keep his relationship clandestine, he might now be a senior figure. This is another example of the Church discouraging honesty among its gay clergy.

It was, however, felt that it was not impossible to be appointed as an archdeacon or a dean, although if one were openly gay it was now impossible to be appointed as a bishop. George asserted that there had been *"quite a flurry"* of single men being appointed as deans during the previous few years, but that since the Jeffrey John uproar, *"there is still a nervousness about appointing single clergy as bishops."*

Media scrutiny was felt to be a significant factor in aggravating this situation. *"I suppose we shouldn't be subject to media scrutiny in that way, but I think the media expect the bishops to be beyond reproach,"* reflected Greg. He did not see other kinds of preferment as being out of the question: *"If it were becoming an archdeacon, I don't think it's a sufficiently high-profile job to say no to. Or even being dean of a cathedral, if any of those sort of jobs came along."* His reasoning was that, if he were to be appointed as a bishop, *"somebody might see you in the media who knows you and wants to be mischievous".*

Grant had received reassurance that he was fairly safe from media attention so long as he did not obtain preferment: *"I did worry a bit that I might be exposed and it might be in the press. You know, 'Priest has lover in mid county village'. And I spoke to my spiritual director about it, and he said, 'Oh, you're not a canon or an archdeacon or a bishop. They won't be worried about you!'"* Of course, if it were not for the Church's prohibition on clergy having gay relationships, there would be little or no media interest in those who do. Such is secular acceptance of gay relationships that those of other public figures are no longer likely to attract headlines.

It seems unlikely that the Church of England will appoint any further gay bishops in the foreseeable future, particularly since the Lambeth Conference of 2008 endorsed the Windsor moratorium on doing so. As Tomlinson writes, "By failing to make controversial appointments the Church of England will deny itself an important source of inspiration and support, indeed some of its potential most celebrated leaders" (2004:37).

Congregational response or "People will cut you almost infinite slack."

Successive polls have suggested that lay people's opinions about whether homosexuals should be ordained are gradually becoming increasingly positive. In discussing with the homosexual interviewees their perceptions of the responses they

had encountered from those amongst whom they had ministered, five themes emerged that suggested allowing clergy to be
in openly gay relationships might be accepted even by some
who, if asked, would express disapproval of such relationships.

Firstly, for some parishioners it was no problem at all. Gareth
recounted that, in one of his parishes, his partner had been in
evidence but *"parishioners just weren't bothered. I mean, one of the
sweet older ladies, who'd never talk about these things, said, 'I'm glad
you've got somebody'."* An elderly lady had said to Guy, *"'Is it so
wrong that we should want the gay people to be happy?'"* He
continued, *"And I thought, 'This is the voice that never gets spoken'."*
Greg's experience was that *"D is here most weekends, and people
know he's around. And at functions, like the Flower Festival, we go and
have lunch together over there. And if I have an event here, D is
around. And we don't make any fuss about it. We just get on with life."*

When his long-term relationship ended, Grant actually found
that his parishioners were supportive: *"I'm not very good at being
Coco the Clown and hiding my feelings. And people in the parish knew
something was up. They knew T was around a lot. And a lot of them
had guessed he was my partner, without it actually being spoken of.
And what it's actually done for me is that a lot of people in leadership
in the church – the churchwardens and some of the people on the PCC
– all know about me now. The pain of the break up has actually helped
me here in the parish, and I've spoken quite honestly about my feelings
to my two churchwardens and the two deputies, and they reckoned that
there are a lot of people in the congregation who, sort of, on a sub-
conscious level, think their vicar may be, but they don't need to voice
it."*

George had been taken aback when he attended a farewell
service for a priest who was leaving a semi-rural parish, and *"the
churchwardens, and indeed the local mayor, said, 'Oh, we're going to
miss Father So-and-so. And of course we're going to miss his partner
as well terribly.' Well, I didn't quite know how to react."*

The second theme was that for some parishioners having a

homosexual vicar was an issue, but they had not pushed any concerns. Giles felt that in parishes, *"the vast majority of people will be perhaps not against but certainly ambivalent about gay sexuality."* Grant had found that a number of the older members of his congregation had voiced negative views about homosexuals without realising his own sexuality: *"I don't think they would know their reasons. It was just their feeling. They are people who are so entrenched in all sorts of things about their faith, that whatever you teach, you're wrong. What Father So-and-so taught them in nineteen fifty-something was correct. Whatever you say isn't. It's all part of a package."*

When Greg's partner began to be seen regularly some years previously, *"I was amazed how quickly the rumours went round here,"* but now *"it's not an issue that's talked about in the village anymore."* George told me that, in his experience, no official complaint had been brought against anyone: *"In my ministry and since I've been a senior clergyman, there have been two occasions when I have received anonymous phone calls from someone who was complaining about their vicar, believing that he was living in a homosexual relationship. But I asked this person to put this in writing, to state the facts and put his name to it, as I needed to share this with the priest myself, which the person refused to do. And I also had an anonymous letter."* If complainants do not wish to pursue their concern by giving their name, he explained, no action can be taken by the Church.

The third theme was that for many parishioners, the vicar's personal life is of no interest. Guy remembered working in a parish of *"very conventional conservative people. But while I was there, I was never once asked by anybody. And I don't think that was necessarily because they all assumed I was straight. I think they weren't interested."* Gavin had felt exposed in a rural parish, although the parishioners *"weren't interested in me in that way. As most people are, they were wrapped up with their own stuff."* Gareth considered that for the congregations amongst whom he ministered, *"it doesn't matter to them whether I'm gay or straight. It's whether I can find my way round an eight o'clock communion, or whether I can get my way through a Family Service or singing and stuff. Actually that's what people want. They don't want to know what I do with my private life."*

The final theme of this dimension was that most parishioners offer tacit acceptance if they have cause to like the clergyman in question. *"I think some people don't want it rubbed in their faces really. They can accept without really acknowledging it. I think some people just don't need to have it named,"* said Grant. Gordon suggested that, although parishioners might use a clergyman's sexuality against him if they had other reasons not to like him, *"essentially, it's not even about being good or bad. If you really love them and try to do what you're meant to do, even if you're rubbish at it, people will cut you almost infinite slack."* As has been shown and will continue to be shown in what follows, the Church goes to great lengths to show disapproval of partnered homosexual clergy. One reason for this given in *Issues* is that clergymen's lives "must be free of anything which will make it difficult for others to have confidence in them" (para 5.14).The experience of the gay interviewees suggests that, as far as the typical parishioner is concerned, a less negative approach by the Church could be considered acceptable.

Consideration for others, or "The sin is disturbing the harmony"

This dimension, which arose from the interviews with the retired clergymen, offers reasoning behind the hypocrisy that is further discussed in the next dimension.

The retired respondents, representing the status quo, were concerned that ordinary parishioners should not be upset. Some recalled the upset that had been caused by allowing women to become priests. Ralph had voted against this, not because he objected in principle, but *"because I felt that the legislation that was being put in place at that time would give us a two-tier priesthood.*

People who were accepted within a small group and those who didn't happen to recognise them." Ronald remembered how distressed some elderly people had been: "*The Holy Spirit was gradually leading towards such a decision being made, and if it had been allowed to continue as a gradual thing, the elderly people who were likely to be upset would have gradually died out before it was passed. The decision was too soon.*"

It was felt that allowing openly homosexual men to become priests also might upset some people. Roderick said, "*The style of life of people living in the vicarage is always known in the community and there could be activities which adversely affect attitudes towards the Church.*" It was Ronald who summed up the general feeling of the retired respondents: "*What happens behind closed doors is people's own business. God is the judge. The sin in my eyes is disturbing the harmony and breaking up the Kingdom of God.*"

Following from these themes was the third one, "People can't be upset if they don't know". Robert paved the way to the concluding dimension by telling me that "*the bishop who ordained me had a very good clear rule about difficult questions: 'It would have been a lot easier if you hadn't asked me. But now you've asked me, I'm about to give you an answer.' I once wrote to him about the fact that I'd got somebody on my church council who I knew perfectly well was living with someone else's wife. And so he said, 'Well I have to write back to you and say you've got to say to them that this brings you into confrontation with accepted moral standards. But I would have preferred it if you hadn't asked the question! I wouldn't have known about it.' And I think that still motivates some bishops.*"

"Don't ask, don't tell" – a long standing approach

Explicitly and implicitly, this phrase features again and again, both in published literature and in the interview material, to encapsulate the ongoing approach of the Church of England to homosexuals. Both Bates and Hampson use it to sum up paragraph 5.18 near the end of *Issues in Human Sexuality*. This states that, although in the light of the report's conclusions "some may propose that bishops should be more rigorous in searching out and exposing clergy who may be in sexually active homophile relationships", this approach is rejected for two reasons: firstly because it should not be assumed that two people of the same sex who live together are in an "erotic relationship", and secondly because a "general inquisition" would infringe the rights of all clergy "who give no occasion for scandal" to be treated with trust and respect. "In other words," says Bates (2005:135), "don't ask, don't tell." Heskins, too, asserts that the Church of England "has managed to get by since the publication of *Issues in Human Sexuality* through an adoption of an unwritten agreement between bishops and gay clergy that the one won't ask if the other doesn't tell" (2005:31).

Significantly, this dimension emerged from both sets of interviews. Among the retired clergymen, four themes make up the dimension. Firstly, it was considered that some bishops are partisan. Ronald thought that this might be because they are themselves following a gay agenda, or it may just be that they are privately sympathetic. At the conference that Roy had attended in the eighties, *"it was clear that the principals didn't disapprove of this – certain principals, you know, certain principals who spoke as if they didn't, and, asked about placing these men, said, 'Well, when the time comes to seek a parish you'll just have to be careful which bishop you approach.' Showing I think that some bishops were in on the thing."*

Secondly it was felt that, for whatever reason, bishops turn a blind eye to an ordinand or priest's sexuality. Richard said that *"Some bishops would prefer 'not to know', and I have every sympathy for them in this way."* Robert agreed: *"I think the majority of bishops, now, prefer not to ask the question. And that's how they cope with it. They work on the basis that if nothing's said..."*

Thirdly, it was suggested that, because bishops don't ask the question, they can proceed unknowingly. Roland spoke of

Archbishop Robert Runcie who *"said that he had ordained homosexual people. I don't know whether he knew that they were practising homosexuals, but he thought they might have been. He wasn't going to ask."* When Roy obtained preferment, *"I said I'm not conducting a witch hunt, nor shall I be, but I will not knowingly put anyone forward for ordination and I will not appoint anybody to a parish, knowing that they are actively homosexual."*

Fourthly, the retired respondents recognised that, because bishops follow the party line, a gay clergyman would be unlikely to tell his bishop about his sexuality. Roger noted, *"The bishop's first task is of course 'pastor for pastors' and supposed to look after the clergy, and it's quite difficult because the person who's supposed to look after you is your boss too."*

Among the homosexual interviewees, four similar themes make up the dimension. The first was that the "Hierarchy don't want to ask and choose not to know". Gordon thought that *"if your life is discreet and you're not overtly campaigning in front of them, they feel that they don't really want to go as far as to confront you, because they would find it a distasteful thing that they wouldn't want to talk about."* *"I think bishops are reluctant to ask basically,"* agreed Greg.

In fact, the interviewees pointed out that bishops have the excuse that they are actually not supposed to ask. Gordon explained with irony that *"the great thing about bishops in Issues in Human Sexuality is the 'You may not enquire'. And bishops of course put that in for a reason, because it's their catch-all. I mean, somebody might say, 'Bishop, that priest in my parish is a lesbian'. And he would say, 'How do you know that?' And they would say, 'Well, you can tell'. And he would then be able to say, 'I'm sorry. We follow Issues in Human Sexuality. You are not to pry into other people's private lives and, unless you have reason to believe that her life is causing scandal, you must back away.'"*

Geoff recounted that *"The bishop's reaction depends on what he officially knows. What bishops don't want to know they as a rule do not know. An infinitesimal series of accommodations are reached between bishops and their clergy. What a bishop knows is influenced on a particular occasion and by why he needs to know it."* Gerald felt that bishops choosing not to notice things that they privately know is *"the usual pattern"*. So it might be, but does this make it acceptable?

The second theme was that the "Hierarchy doesn't want it talked about". Grant had worked in an area where the bishop was *"obviously a gay man"*, but *"it was never known about and never talked about. So I was his chaplain in an area where there were a lot of gay clergy, some of them with partners. It was 'don't know, don't tell', you know."* Graham told me that, in the past, *"All the bishops have been to dinner with R and myself. But they ignored it. This was the crazy way that things were done; you don't talk about it."* And Gus recounted that *"a great friend of mine whispered to the bishop the other day, 'Bishop, you know I'm homosexual, don't you?' And he said, 'Yes, but don't broadcast it'... I think that's always been the case, and rather sadly I think it still is the case really."*

When Guy was about to be ordained, his bishop was keen that he should not talk about his sexuality. *"He said, 'You have the option. You can either be up front and noisy and there'll be 2% of the parishes in the Church of England that you might be able to work in. Or you can be quiet and discreet and you've got 98% of parishes you could work in.'"* Guy's observations about the *"rules of silence"* enforced by the Church endorsed comments made to Jeffrey Heskins by his gay clergy interviewees, many of whom, Heskins reports, "said that it was an uphill struggle to live honestly in a Church context that seemed to be complicit with secrecy and punitive of openness" (2005:177).

As regards the third theme, it will already be evident that examples given by the interviewees indicated that the "Hierarchy has practised 'don't ask, don't tell' for a long time". As mentioned in the previous chapter, when speaking of the years before the Higton Debate, Gerald, speaking from experience, suggested that at that time it was not difficult to find a bishop who would appoint a gay clergyman *"on the 'don't ask, don't tell' basis"* so long as he fulfilled the necessary criteria. George agreed that the approach was far from new: *"Gay clergy know that I know, but I don't approach them about it. And I think that's been the practice for a very long time."* Such hypocrisy, then, seems to have become accepted practice in the Church.

The final theme both complements the retired respondents' final theme and also indicates sympathy on the part of the homosexual clergy for the situation in which bishops find themselves. Regarding his own situation, Gerald colluded with the Church in its approach: *"It's a matter of 'don't ask, don't tell.' There's no reason why the Bishop should know that I'm in a civil partnership."* Asked whether he thought many bishops do ask clergy about the physical side of their civil partnerships, Gareth replied, *"I think that's difficult. I can't imagine it can be much fun to have to ask those questions."* Graham said that he had tried never to tell a bishop anything that would put the bishop in an uncomfortable position. One reason for gay clergy's toleration of the Church's approach, then, is that they have a fundamental respect for their bishops and do not want to cause awkwardness for them.

Nicholas Coulton (2005) points out the contradiction of *Some Issues in Human Sexuality* claiming that the Church is willing to listen to the experience of gay people, yet, in forbidding clergy to be in homosexual partnerships, ruling out the possibility that these men can contribute to such a process. The endorsement of *Issues in Human Sexuality*'s conclusion makes frank discussion of homosexuality risky even for lay people in same-sex partnerships. The pressure to remain "clandestine", he continues, subjects homosexual partnerships to unnatural pressure, making them less likely to be enduring.

For Marilyn McCord Adams, the approach of the Church is to treat homosexuality as taboo. Taboos, she maintains, "are enemies of Christian discernment insofar as they try to maintain social order through inarticulate fear". Taboo-approaches to sexuality "tend to keep everyone in the closet as sexual persons". She concludes that Christians are called to bring every part of themselves, including their sexual relationships "out in the open with God" in order to discern divine approval or otherwise. "In the absence of established institutions", she continues, how else are gay Christians "to arrive at wholesome patterns of life together except by trying experiments and praying them through?"(2005:36-48)

Since that was written, civil partnership has not only come into being but also has become established as a way in which same-sex couples can gain legal recognition of their relationship. Publicly proclaiming a relationship in this way results in support not only from friends and family but also from the community in general. Such support is bound to increase the possibility of the relationship lasting. Although the Church has had little option but to tolerate this, since it is part of the law of the land, the traditional teaching that any sexual activity outside marriage is wrong makes it impossible for physically expressed same-sex relationships, however faithful, stable or legal, to be blessed or recognised. The House of Bishops' requirement that clergy entering civil partnerships should be celibate ensures that the double standards of 'don't ask, don't tell' remain necessary if embarrassment and scandal are to be avoided.

CHAPTER 5

THE PROBLEM OF CIVIL PARTNERSHIPS

Most people would surely agree that, if one is lucky enough to find someone with whom to share mutual love, respect and trust, being in a committed relationship with them is likely to benefit the happiness, security and health of both parties. Gay people were naturally delighted when it became possible in 2005 to acknowledge their relationships publicly and legally by formalising them in civil partnerships. Living in a civil partnership is now a universally recognised alternative to being married, single or divorced, and indeed was included with these options on the latest census form.

However, the Church of England's continued insistence that, for clergy in particular, sexual activity should take place only within the context of marriage, presented the hierarchy with the problem of how to respond to this new legal development. The contributions from the gay interviewees presented in this chapter make clear that in 2005 the Church began to engage in further forms of hypocrisy in order to address this difficulty. It should be noted that this study was conducted before the Government's proposal to introduce gay marriage and the subsequent negative response from the Church. No specific mention is therefore made of this development, although much of this chapter is relevant to it.

Traditionally the texts in Genesis concerning God's creation of man and woman have been taken to mean that the marriage of a man and woman and their subsequent fruitfulness is clearly the natural order ordained by God. *Some Issues in Human Sexuality* re-emphasises the conventional position that Genesis 2:24 provides "a blueprint for monogamous heterosexual marriage" because "this is the human social institution that gives public expression to the ideal of a permanent and exclusive union between one man and one woman" (para 3.4.65). This in turn "provides the benchmark by which to assess all the various alternative forms of sexual activity and relationship that the Old Testament describes" (para 3.4.75).

An aspect of marriage which has remained constant in the teaching of the Church is the image of it as a sign of the covenant between God and His people, or between Christ and his Church. The Old Testament uses this image in the story of Hosea, which symbolizes God's faithfulness in the face of Israel's idolatry. The New Testament takes up this theme in the symbolism of Christ's self-sacrifice because of his love for his people. Marriage is seen as a sacrament that reflects the great mystery of salvation.

However, during the last few decades, various changes have taken place in the Church's approach to marriage that would seem to lead it closer to the possibility that a faithful homosexual partnership could be regarded as similarly sacramental. Changing ideas of what constitute the purposes of matrimony are reflected in changes to the Marriage Service. While the Book of Common Prayer declares the primary aim to be procreation, the Common Worship liturgy cites first the bringing together of the couple in the "delight and tenderness of sexual union and joyful commitment to the end of their lives", before describing marriage as the "foundation of family life". In modern marriage, the personal relationship between the couple has become increasingly emphasised over the institutional and economic aspects which were once of vital importance. In addition, equality of the two partners has become the norm. No longer is the male the superior to be obeyed.

Thus, traditional teaching about marriage has been adapted to reflect modern values. Another such development is in the Church of England's official stance on divorce and remarriage. While its position is still that God's intention is that marriage should be for life, the pastoral realities which were being faced by clergy led to a relaxation of the ban on remarriage in church. It was in 1981 that the General Synod accepted the principle that remarriage of divorced people should be permitted By doing so, Synod was showing acceptance of the increasingly influential view of marriage as a relationship which in reality can break down. In 1985, a service of blessing after a civil marriage of divorced people was approved by the House of Bishops, and in 1990, the bar on ordination for remarried people was removed. Finally, in 2002, Synod allowed that there are exceptional situations in which divorced people should be allowed to marry in church during the lifetime of a former partner. *Some Issues* explains that this position recognises that there are "circumstances in which this is the best Christian response to a less than ideal situation" (para 1.2.48).

While it is arguable whether a homosexual partnership should be described as "a less than ideal situation", there do seem to be parallels that the Church might take into account in its present ban on any form of blessing of such a partnership. Now that secular civil partnership is entirely accepted legally, such a ban is out of step with pastoral realities as civil partnerships are increasingly entered by parishioners. Moreover, it has led to the necessity for further hypocrisy on the part of the Church hierarchy in order to cope with the number of its clergy who enter them.

Civil Partnership: The Church's official line and the reality

Rowan Williams, in the Michael Harding memorial address he delivered to the Lesbian and Gay Christian Movement in 1989, explored a theology which led to the conclusion that sexuality is sacramental and sexual relationships occasions of 'grace'. Concluding that there is in the Bible "a good deal to steer us away from assuming that reproductive sex is a norm" (2002:11), Williams makes it clear that he does not believe the expression of sexual love should be limited to heterosexual marriage.

Despite Rowan Williams' views, publications issued by the House of Bishops during his archiepiscopacy, *Some Issues in Human Sexuality* and the pastoral statement issued just before the Civil Partnership Act came into force, maintain that the Church's teaching on sexual ethics remains unchanged. Marriage is defined as the lifelong union between a man and a woman, and for Christians, marriage is the only proper context for a sexual relationship. This position obliged the House of Bishops to insist in their 2005 pastoral statement that a clergyman who entered a civil partnership would be required to assure his bishop that the relationship was "consistent with the standards for the clergy set out in *Issues in Human Sexuality*" (para 19), in other words that it was celibate.

Once again, a statement had been issued on behalf of the hierarchy which did not express the principles of individual bishops. Writing in the Church Times (August 19th 2005) soon after the pastoral statement was issued, the Rt. Revd. Peter Selby lamented that it "should be a source not of fear, but of delight, that many who do not aspire to matrimony, or to whose circumstances it is inappropriate, wish none the less to order their lives by means of as many of the aspects of the married state are made available to them." He expresses the hope that bishops "will find better ways of relating" to clergy entering civil partnerships than to seek the assurances of celibacy that the pastoral statement requires.

Of the homosexual interviewees, most had either already entered into civil partnerships or had long-term partners with whom they were considering doing so. They had significant views and experiences to offer about the policy contained in the bishops' pastoral statement and the reality of how this operates.

These men wanted to be able to live with their partner in the same open, accepted way as their heterosexual colleagues. However, as Geoff explained, *"The problem is that there is no way of normalising a relationship within the church. The only way then of conducting one is in a clandestine way."* Graham was aware that the gay world is often perceived as being promiscuous, *"and I say, 'Well, you make it promiscuous, if you won't allow a partner, an openly blessed partner.'"*

Heterosexual relationships are stabilised by marriage, it was suggested. Guy acknowledged that he had had a number of partners, but *"if I'd been allowed to marry, I might have operated relationships in a different way."* The possibility of marriage, he considered, *"brings you to a point of deciding exactly what your commitment is, and it clarifies things very sharply.... Where there's no framework and structure, where there's not marriage to run away from, it can make you too serious when you're young. You have to invent your own morality."*

The pastoral statement by the House of Bishops issued when the socially acceptable structure of civil partnerships became a reality was described by Guy as ludicrous and offensive. Asked whether he and his partner had been required by their bishop to give any assurances of celibacy when they entered their civil partnership, as suggested by the pastoral statement, Gavin replied emphatically that they had not and would not have done so: *"That would be deeply patronising."*

Not only did the data from the homosexual interviewees suggest that the Church's official line on civil partnerships encourages furtiveness, it also showed that, hypocritically, the line is not in fact being adhered to. *"I know a number of clergy who have entered civil partnerships,"* said Grant. Gerald also declared that *"actually an awful lot of priests have done it now, quietly,"* and that *"the Church of England, as usual, in the end, tends to come to a fairly sort of sensible, pragmatic position on these things."* This position seems to be another variation of 'don't ask, don't tell'.

Are bishops asking for an assurance of celibacy from these priests, as required by the pastoral statement? *"Right from the start, a number of bishops pretty well openly declared that they weren't going to operate it,"* asserted Gerald. After Gavin's civil partnership, his partner, also a priest, *"wrote on the vicar's advice to the diocesan bishop, who then said, 'Ok, that's fine, but you should have let us know before you were actually doing it'. That was the first point that was made. 'But I want you to go and have a conversation with the Bishop of X.' We were happy to do that. He is quite a good friend of ours, and knows us both, and that we live together and has been to have dinner with us. So I went to have a conversation with him, and that was that. But there were no difficult questions."*

When Gordon entered his civil partnership, he wrote to tell his bishop. The reply sent warm good wishes for the day of the ceremony from both the suffragan and diocesan bishops, and stated, *"'We understand that there is a letter on file saying that you intend to lead your ministry in accordance with Issues in Human Sexuality. Therefore we can have no problem with it at all.'"* Gordon was initially baffled by this, but concluded that *"when I was ordained, the bishops involved basically in a rather cursory way said 'You do understand that we would expect you to lead your life by the spirit of what's in Issues in Human Sexuality?' And I must have said, 'Yes.'"* Gordon showed me the letter he had received from his bishop, who, when appointed to a new position soon afterwards, was quoted in the press as being committed to *Issues*. There was no suggestion in the letter that any questions needed to be asked or answered.

Same-sex blessings: The Church's official line and the reality

The bishops' pastoral statement declares that "the House of Bishops affirms that clergy of the Church of England should not provide services of blessing for those who register a civil partnership" (para 17). It was felt by some interviewees to be an anomaly that civil partnerships cannot be blessed when so many seemingly less significant things can. *"I used to think it was so awful that people were blessing a Trident nuclear warship, but you weren't actually allowed to bless something that's given with grace,"* lamented Grant. Gareth agreed: *"I do have problems when clergy are asked to bless the sea, or they will bless fields, or they bless animals. And I've heard that Army chaplains will bless weapons. So I do find it odd. You land up blessing rings, and buildings and homes and things. So it seems strange that we can't pray for two people to grow more in their faith and in their relationship and love for each other."*

However, despite the fact that blessing same-sex unions has never been allowed, such ceremonies have evidently been happening for years. Graham told me that he had quietly been conducting such services of blessing since 1969. Giles stated that about fifteen years previously he had been asked to *"assist liturgically"* in a service of blessing for two lesbians. The person presiding has since obtained preferment, and *"now of course that he's a senior bishop, it's a very different story."* In other words, having become a bishop, this man too felt obliged to repress any prior feelings of support for gay people and to follow the party line.

Since the introduction of civil partnerships, blessings have continued to take place. George asserted that *"in London there are a huge percentage of civil partnerships which are seen as gay marriages and are recognised as such by some clergy, and have been blessed by some clergy."* In 2008, media publicity was attracted by a service of blessing for two priests at St Bartholomew the Great, Smithfield, and by the reprimand that was issued to the presiding priest by both Archbishops and the Bishop of London.

Giles recounted, *"We went to one [service of blessing] only last summer of two priests, both friends of mine. They signed the civil partnership back in May and then in August they had a public service in their parish church, presided over by their parish priest, which to all intents and purposes was just like a wedding. They had a choir, they had organ music, there was incense, it was a mass. The words that were used, exchanging vows and the blessing and everything else. It was lovely. But I think it surprised us as to how open it was."*

Blessings were evidently popular. When Graham took them,

the parents of the couple would often say, *"'I wish my wedding had been like this'. Because we made the service tailor-made to the couple who came, choosing the readings and the words that they said to each other."* Giles commented on the fact that at same-sex blessings, people would come who had never been in a church before, and therefore what positive occasions they were: *"The church was doing what it should do: welcoming in people on the margins."* Both Graham and Greg had stopped conducting these services because they found it difficult to cope with the large demand for them.

Thus, despite the ban on blessing same-sex unions, they have happened and continue to happen. The reality is that the bishops' guidelines are not infrequently ignored. Bishops seem happy to turn a blind eye unless media attention is attracted: another example of double standards.

Civil Partnership: "He is my partner, not my husband" or Not Marriage

There has been much heated discussion since David Cameron's government proposed to introduce gay marriage. As the interviewees could not have foreseen that such proposals would be made, this concept was not discussed at their interviews. They did, however, discuss the relationship of civil partnership to marriage.

Perhaps surprisingly in view of recent statements from advocates of gay marriage, the homosexual interviewees were agreed that not only was civil partnership not the same theological concept as marriage, but also that they would not want it to be perceived as such.

"I think I guessed, when this was on the horizon, that this would be interpreted as gay marriage, and it has been. It was only a matter of hours from when we had the first civil partnerships that the media were reporting them as such," said George. The term "gay weddings", with or without inverted commas, was used in newspapers

ranging in style from the *Daily Express* to *The Times* when the first civil partnerships were signed in December 2005.

However, although they believed civil partnership was similar in quality to marriage, the homosexual interviewees did not feel this word was an appropriate one to use. *"It's not a word I would use. I would use the word "marriage" as an analogy. I would say it's analogous to marriage, but it's very clear that marriage is something that happens between a man and a woman,"* said Gavin. Graham agreed: *"It's an entirely different relationship from marriage. It's got similarities... With two men or two women, the dynamics are usually quite different."* Both he and Giles felt that one of the essential differences was the inability of a same-sex couple to procreate. Nevertheless, Giles continued, *"I think that in the eyes of God, it's very similar to marriage."*

The factor that made it similar was commitment. *"What matters to my mind is the quality of the relationship. What matters is the quality of any relationship,"* said Gavin. When preparing heterosexual couples for marriage, Grant would ask himself how their relationship equated to his own, and came up with the answer that *"all relationships are sacramental."* Giles stated that *"in the same way in which married people believe that the arrangement they have is permanent, we would believe that of ourselves as well. And in fact in many cases, more permanent than marriage. I mean, we see these days how dissoluble marriage is, and the huge rate of divorce and all that sort of thing. We know gay couples who have been in relationships for 15, 20, 25, 30 years."*

While not being marriage, civil partnership is similar not only in quality but also in legality, it was asserted. *"I think I've defended civil partnerships by saying that actually it* isn't *marriage,"* said Grant, explaining, *"All it is is acknowledging a partnership for legal rights and pension rights."* Giles was considering undertaking a civil partnership, and reasoned, *"in terms of just making an act of commitment which is recognised in law, perhaps in terms of giving each of us next of kin rights should one of us be critically ill in hospital or something, it would be useful from that point of view."*

With regard to suitable terminology, Graham said, *"The word 'marriage' conjures up wedding veils and mothers crying in the front row, you know. I think 'partnership' is perhaps a better word really, civil partnership. When I'm asked about R, I say he's my civil partner. I don't like husband and wife. He isn't my husband."*

Gus agreed that, as long as the term 'civil partnership' is used, it gives the lie to *"these tiresome people who say that it is marriage, and 'It's undermining marriage' and things like that."* Gareth had a high opinion of marriage, which, despite supporting civil partnerships, he did not want to see undermined: *"I want the Church to uphold marriage and the family as important roles in society. Most gay people grew up in a normal family. It's been an important place for them to grow and to learn to be, in relationship."*

Whatever the terminology used, it was clear that commitment, stability and permanence were seen by the gay interviewees as values to aspire to as much in a homosexual partnership as in a heterosexual one. It might reasonably be expected that the Church would applaud this ideal and offer its support to gay couples in their efforts to achieve it. However, such is its fear of being seen to defend the physical expression of these couples' love that it continues to withhold its blessing even now homosexual unions are legal.

Thus the advent of civil partnerships has caused the Church to engage in further forms of hypocrisy in order to maintain its traditional position as society's attitudes increasingly emphasise what might be thought to be biblical principles of justice. It has been shown in this chapter that, although guidelines have been issued by the House of Bishops about procedure when faced with priests entering civil partnerships, these guidelines are largely ignored in a new form of "don't ask, don't tell". The ban on blessing ceremonies, too, is not infrequently flouted, and the determination of the Church to maintain this ban is yet another way in which it is out of step with modern British society.

Concluding the exploration of the hypocrisy that, it is contended, characterises the approach of the Church of England hierarchy to their homosexual clergy, the next chapter considers this hypocrisy in the context of the very different position of secular homosexuals today from their counterparts in 1967.

CHAPTER 6

DIVERGENCE FROM SOCIETY

Until relatively recently, many homosexuals felt it necessary to live very circumspectly in order to avoid harassment in their communities and workplaces. Legal reforms, however, notably the Equality Act (Sexual Orientation) Regulations of 2007, have liberated secular homosexuals from any need to be discreet. No longer do they need to fear discrimination of any kind. Their sexuality cannot be used to dismiss them or deny them promotion. They can introduce their partners openly at social events and nonchalantly book double rooms on holiday.

Ironically, as life for the secular homosexual has become simpler, life for the gay clergyman has become more problematic. As society's attitudes have become more liberal, so official Church of England pronouncements have become more determinedly conservative. At the same time, people in general have become more aware of homosexuals and so, while at one time a partner could easily be passed off as just a friend, that is no longer the case. A single clergyman is likely to be suspected now of being homosexual, where once it would be thought that he was committed to celibacy.

The focus of this chapter is the contention that taking such a radically different stance on the issue of homosexuality from that of secular society constitutes yet another form of hypocrisy.

The dimension "A Different World" emerged from my analysis both of the retired heterosexual respondents' interview contributions and of those of the gay clergymen. Both groups identified ways in which the current secular world differed from that of 1967 which had significance for the homosexual Christian. How each group presented and viewed these differences varied, which is why the same dimension is presented twice, a discrete subtitle each time indicating the differing perspective of the retired heterosexuals and the homosexuals.

The final dimension of this chapter, "A Different Church", explores changes in the Church during the forty-year period. Whereas "A Different World" presents changes in society which have been predominantly positive for the secular homosexual, "A Different Church" presents changes in the Church of England and the wider Church which have been correspondingly negative for the homosexual Christian and particularly for the homosexual clergyman.

Through the discussion of changing attitudes during the forty-year period, the chapter illustrates that, whereas in 1967 attitudes in the Church to homosexuality were in line with those of society, in 2007 they were diametrically opposite. While the House of Bishops, despite private views of individual members, would collectively no doubt contend that the Church is holding out against a secular slide into moral decay, the chapter argues that, by refusing to accommodate the changes in secular attitudes, the Church is arguably closing its eyes to the way God is working through these and is certainly denying social justice, thereby contradicting its own mission.

A Different World, or "Constant liberalisation"

The retired heterosexual respondents, having been adults in 1967, were in the better collective position to compare the attitudes of society to homosexuality at the beginning of the forty-year period with those at the end. The word "liberalisation" was used by many of these respondents, often in a less than positive way.

Five themes emerged. The first was "From Homosexuals are Criminals to Homosexuals are our Friends". It was believed that the passing of the Sexual Offences Act in 1967, decriminalising homosexuality, marked the beginning of social change. Ralph referred to the film 'Victim', released in 1961: This featured Dirk

Bogarde portraying a successful barrister who was one of the victims of a ring blackmailing homosexuals. It was the first English language film to use the word "homosexual". Ralph remembered *"that had a great effect on the people I spoke to at that time and particularly in connection to the decriminalisation of homosexuality."* Roy saw public sympathies change during the sixties: *"I suspect that many people would have thought, all right, in the secular world, you know, if that's what people want, then it shouldn't be a criminal offence."* By 2007, public awareness and acceptance of homosexuals had grown enormously. Robert remarked, *"Time has rolled on a lot since the law changed. Most people nowadays, unless they walk round with their eyes and ears totally shut, must be aware that somebody in their office has got a boyfriend or a girlfriend."* In other words, homosexuals are recognised and accepted members of society.

The second theme was "From Strict Sexual Values to The Permissive Society". The retired respondents had been brought up to be sexually abstinent before marriage. Robert explained that, because the Pill was not available and there were strict rules about women sleeping in male college rooms, he and his wife did not sleep together until they married. Clergymen would not dream of having to deal with homosexual issues, but did expect to offer guidance to people experiencing problems arising from the aforementioned circumstances. Robin's example of a parishioner's great distress at the pregnancy of her unmarried daughter describes a situation that would barely raise an eyebrow today. Now, with unmarried couples openly living together, *"What had been the only meaning of sin became no sin at all,"* he said.

As far as homosexuality was concerned, society had gone "From Seeing it Nowhere to Seeing it Everywhere", which constituted the third theme. There was a lack of awareness of it amongst most people in 1967. *"I think a lot of people didn't even know it was going on,"* said Roger. This lack of awareness led to naivety on the part of the public: *"If the vicar had a lodger in the vicarage, I think it was just assumed that it would help to pay the rent and so on,"* recalled Roy. People just accepted that homosexual acts were immoral because they were illegal, explained Roland, adding, *"But they didn't go round looking for them."*

Conversely, *"Today it's assumed if you're single and you're living like that, that you must be up to something not quite right,"* said Roy of same-sex couples. He recalled with amusement a holiday with a male friend who was a missionary, during which they had taken a photograph of themselves in their room: *"I mean can you imagine today – a photo of the bishop and a missionary in bed together!"* The media's eagerness to publicise homosexual relationships between people in the public eye has added to society's greatly heightened awareness of the possibility that two friends of the same sex may be in such a relationship.

"From We Defer to Authority to We Think for Ourselves" was the fourth theme. It explained changes in attitude both to religious leaders and to the Bible. *"I think there's been a whole change in public attitude to people in positions of authority. I think that the Prime Minister or the Queen or the Archbishop of Canterbury would not have been slated in the way that is often done in the press nowadays,"* said Ralph. He felt that this change had come about *"partly through education. It seems to me that children are encouraged to question everything."*

In the final theme, the retired respondents identified the shift "From We don't know any Homosexuals in the Church to What are we going to do about Homosexuals in the Church?" Robin explained why homosexuals in the Church were not recognised, asking, *"Forty years ago, would I have known of a parishioner's sexuality? Because it was an imprisonable offence. If you had those inclinations, you kept them very well covered. And if two young men lodged together, that was what it was. You didn't assume anything else."* It was agreed that it was the advent of Gay Liberation campaigning that, as Roland put it, *"forced society and forced the*

Church to look at this issue." This was generally seen as a negative move. Ronald believed, *"There is a great liberalisation in the Church which says that anything goes."*

These then are the views of those who were brought up and conducted their ministries within the traditions that the Church of England continues officially to uphold, and who represent the generation that still makes up a significant proportion of congregations. The gay clergymen had great respect for colleagues and parishioners of this generation, recognising that they were accustomed to a world in which homosexuality was taboo. They were anxious that such people should not be upset by having homosexuality thrust upon them, and displayed sensitivity when explaining that their wish to protect older members of the Church was one reason for not being overt about their sexuality. The gay clergymen, too, noted the significant changes in the world since 1967, but their observations brought out different emphases.

A Different World, or "Everything is possible but nothing is forgivable"

Rowan Williams coined the subtitle of this dimension, as a description of today's society, in a talk he gave at Great St Mary's Church, Cambridge, on February 22nd 2008. The phrase sums up the gay clergymen's perception of their position in the Church in the light of the changes in secular attitudes to homosexuality outlined in the previous dimension.

The first of the three themes that made up this dimension was "Gays are Cool, except in the Church". It was agreed that homosexuality is not a problem amongst people who are young or even middle-aged. It was contended that young people think that it is odd that anyone would find the idea problematic. In fact, as Gordon suggested, *"A lot of young people think it's rather cool."* Even the middle-aged, he commented, have grown up in a world *"where people aren't frightened of the subject."*

Graham indicated various ways which show the level of acceptance of homosexuals by society. For example, he felt that *"the Press are not so anti as they were. I mean, after the 1987 debate, the headlines were terrible – 'Pulpit poofs to stay' and that sort of thing. And you were very frightened the News of the World would turn up and start ferreting around. I think now, it's not any big deal, unless a clergyman seduces somebody, or, you know, is a paedophile. Well then of course you will get, quite rightly, condemnation from the Press, or exposure. But ordinary clergy with partners – I don't think that really the Press are that interested anymore."* He also pointed out that, whereas if homosexuals wanted a gay social life in the past they were limited to *"seedy, exclusive clubs, I'm so thrilled when I go through Soho now. There are gay bars, gay restaurants, people on the streets, you know. All relaxing as you would if you were heterosexual really."*

In other words, in secular society homosexuality is for the most part treated as no different from heterosexuality. This highlights how far behind the Church has been left in its attitudes. *"There have been advances in society at large in a way that has left the Church of England high and dry,"* said Geoff. Grant recounted that he had recently been to a meeting of the organisation Changing Attitude, who have lost a lot of their lottery funding and other major grants. At the meeting, he heard that *"the reason they haven't got the funding now is that a lot of the more secular funders think everything's been achieved in society now, with civil partnerships here. It's only the silly old Church that's so backward."*

The second theme, "The once unacceptable no problem at all", illustrates that the Church has managed to accommodate other areas of change in society. Gerald remembered relatives forty years ago who *"would not receive into their house as social guests, people who had divorced and married again. I mean, that has changed so quickly, and I think it is a wonderful example of the pragmatism of the Church of England. The way we've accommodated the changing pattern of the way marriages are organised in society."* Such pragmatism does not, however, extend to homosexuality.

The final theme of this dimension "But Society will find you out!" demonstrates that, far from making their lives easier, the acceptance of homosexuals in the secular world has actually made gay clergymen's lives more difficult. As the retired respondents identified, society has changed from being completely naïve about homosexuals to assuming that any close friends of the same sex must be in a relationship. Therefore, whereas it used to be possible for gay clergymen to have a partner without this being realised, it is now necessary to be extremely circumspect, since simply being single is likely to attract unwanted attention. *"The degree of discretion needed has increased. It has become increasingly difficult to expect a person's space to be respected, because society tends to jump to conclusions much more easily today,"* said Geoff.

The contrast between the positive and the negative aspects of society's acceptance was illustrated by Grant's observation: *"On my better days, I like to think there's a culture of honesty in our society, but on my more cynical days, I think there is a more prurient, inappropriate obsession with people's private affairs."* In other words, "Everything is possible but nothing is forgivable".

A further observation about today's society was made by Gareth: *"We're in a culture which is very keen on people presenting themselves. It's very ego centred. And I don't think that's healthy for anybody. Because if you put yourself on a pedestal, or allow other people to do it, you're going to fall."* The gay clergymen interviewed had no desire to be put on a pedestal. Most were wary of preferment. However, they felt that, partly as a result of the double standard in the conclusion of *Issues*, the Church had placed all clergy on one, and that they were therefore fair game to be knocked from it by prurient society.

In any other job, it would not matter at all if a same-sex partnership was detected, and indeed such a partnership would probably be conducted quite openly, so that there would be no need to fear those seeking scandal. However, because of the prohibition in the Church, it is essential that homosexual relationships are kept clandestine. It is remarkable that so many clergymen are prepared to live in such a covert way, and no wonder that Giles was prepared to renounce the prospect of preferment rather than do so.

A Different Church, or "Not the same church as the one that I was ordained into"

In the sixties, as Graham pointed out, the situation for homosexuals in the Church was no different from their situation in the secular world. There was a need for total discretion in both. Today, however, as has been shown, the two circumstances are completely different. There is no need for any discretion in society, while in the Church the need for discretion has increased. On this issue, arguably as on no other apart perhaps from the role of women, the Church is now completely at odds with society. Four themes made up this dimension, and together they indicate the gay interviewees' views, most of them negative, about how the situation in the Church has changed.

The first theme was "Church versus Society". Gareth suggested that the reason the Church's stance on homosexuality is so at variance with that of society is that the Church is striving to survive and that it feels that holding out against the sexual values of the world will help it to achieve this: *"You know, they think it will solve the problem if we just purify the church. And I think they've lost perspective."*

The second theme was "No Longer a Broad Church". It was considered that the Church of England is no longer the broad church that it traditionally was. *"It seems that the Church now is predominantly run by evangelicals - bishops and others... A large number of bishops appointed during George Carey's time were all evangelicals. And since that time I think the balance of the Church of*

England being a broad church has been very significantly redressed," asserted Giles. Gavin too felt that the power of the evangelical wing has unbalanced the way decisions are made.

The third theme was "Global Polarisation". A significant factor in the rise in the Church of England of the wing that condemns homosexual practice is the emergence of members of the Anglican Communion to whom such practice is abhorrent. *"Where did the Anglican Communion suddenly come from?"* asked Guy. *"It never used to matter at a local level. It was a nice jolly every ten years when all the bishops used to come along and say, 'We're being very Anglican in Angola.' 'Oh are you? How nice. Well, we're being frightfully Anglican in Tibet'. Well, well done, everybody! And everyone would go home."* The reason for the increased profile of the Communion in this debate was outlined by Gordon. He asserted that Michael Ramsey's actions would not have had *"such international ramifications as what Rowan Williams does. Because of communications. It's a much smaller world. Obviously the church in Africa was not so ascendant. And it was still in a colonial period, where most of the bishops in Africa would have been western, white guys… The church in Africa was still then very much a satellite of western Christianity."*

The fact that the rise in a liberal attitude to homosexuality both in society and in some sections of the Church coincided with the change in governance of African provinces from colonial primates to men brought up within a deep cultural abhorrence of homosexuality has certainly aggravated the situation. The Anglican Communion has traditionally been held together by strong shared bonds, often covered by the term "bonds of affection". Such bonds have been severely strained by heated expressions of the extreme divergence of views on this issue amongst different provinces; so much so that at the Primates' Meetings both at Dromantine in 2005 and at Dar-es-Salaam in 2007 some primates, notably Archbishop Peter Akinola of Nigeria, refused to take part in the Eucharist. This was because they refused to share in the sacrament with the

Presiding Bishop of the Episcopal Church following the consecration of Gene Robinson. Such conduct would seem not only to break the bonds of affection, but also the constraints of courtesy.

Guy recognised, not altogether sympathetically, that Rowan Williams' position as head of the increasingly disparate Anglican Communion made it impossible for him to adhere to his own liberal views publicly: *"As Archbishop he has to play Archbishop, and that means that he is some sort of spiritual figurehead for the worldwide Anglican Communion. And as such he can't say things which are going to be offensive to the majority of Anglican worshippers."* From this stems Williams' deference to primates such as Archbishop Akinola, and his concern to display understanding of the views of those who have subsequently attended the Global Anglican Future Conference.

A consideration of the archiepiscopacy of Rowan Williams generated the fourth theme, "A Challenged Archbishop". Williams was deemed to be a more accessible archbishop that any of his predecessors, and this affected both his leadership and people's reactions to him. Earlier archbishops, such as Donald Coggan and Robert Runcie, were judged by Gordon to have been *"terribly grand churchmen who hadn't really been in parishes."* He claimed that *"Robert Runcie was known to have a very liberal personal position, absolutely, in an old-fashioned English kind of way. But only the inner circle knew that."* Conversely, he noted that Rowan Williams *"is probably one of the most known Archbishops of Canterbury"*, because he has lived amongst students, has been part of various liberation movements and has *"taught vast amounts of the clergy of the Church of England."* Williams' liberal views have therefore always been well known to many people, as have his friendships with gay clergymen such as Jeffery John.

Far from causing him to lead the Church in a more liberal direction, however, the fact that his views were previously so well known, and indeed severely criticised by the evangelical wing on his appointment, has resulted in Rowan Williams seeming to compensate by deferring to the conservatives. Gordon explained that this is because *"he has a very high Episcopal theology... Which is why he struggles. Instead of talking to the primate of Nigeria and saying, 'You're an absolute bloody disgrace', he struggles for unity, because he believes it's his calling as an archbishop, to be the focus of unity."*

Guy expressed this less sympathetically: *"I think one of our problems as a church is that the bishops have started to believe that they are something special and that there is an office they occupy that must be respected, and which is somehow different from them... And I think Rowan resisted it when he was made a bishop and I think he resisted it when he was made an archbishop, but I think when he was made Archbishop of Canterbury, I think he's fallen into the trap of thinking that he was appointed as someone to shape himself to the office instead of a person who could shape the office by his personality."* In other words, when appointed to the hierarchy of the Church, more than one man has felt obliged to assent to the existing stance on this issue, and to suppress his personal views rather than honestly trying to change the Church's position to one which he privately believes to be just.

Many of the gay interviewees expressed admiration for Rowan Williams as a theologian and as a man, but they were disappointed that, in his desire to maintain unity, he has not remained true to the liberal views which raised homosexuals' hopes on his appointment. The former Bishop of Newark, John Shelby Spong, expressed a similar view in the Church Times (October 30th 2009), "I have affection for Rowan personally, but I do not respect his leadership. One cannot unify the Church by rejecting, or allowing others in the Church, to victimise any child of God [sic]. I really don't expect leadership from representatives of the institutional Church... They are too busy preserving the institution."

This claim is born out by a statement that Jeffery John alleges a bishop made to him in a private discussion about the situation for homosexuals in the Church. In a sermon preached at St Edward's Church, Cambridge on October 18th 2009, John claimed that this bishop said, "You see, Jeffery, bishops don't have the luxury of being able to tell the truth... Their job is to hold the whole show together." Spong, in the article cited above, expressed the belief that "a bishop must use the power of [his] office to contend with evil wherever it appears, either in Church or in society, and never hesitate because the price of contending is too high." This is surely a view with which any Christian should agree.

Graham and Gus were ordained in the fifties and sixties and had witnessed many changes. They were disappointed that the positive changes for homosexuals in society had not been reflected in the Church. Gus said of the negative preoccupation with homosexuality in recent years, *"When I think how my own Church of England, which I now have little time for - it's not the same church as the one that I was ordained into – snaps this up, I think it's absolutely dreadful."* Graham said of the situation for homosexuals in the Church during the last forty years, *"I honestly don't think the Church has changed very much really... I do feel rather gloomy about the future, but I'm not going to be around am I?"*

Hopefully, the future is not as gloomy as Graham feared. The Church of England has managed to accommodate many changes in society, and not only during the period covered by the study. If members of the hierarchy begin to stand up for what they really believe in relation to the theological acceptability of committed, faithful relationships, refusing to be intimidated by vociferous conservatives, there will be more potential for the Church to accommodate the changed understanding and acceptance of homosexuality that has occurred in the secular world. Not only will it then be possible for homosexuals in such relationships to take as full and open a part in the life of the Church as they can in society, but the Church itself will arguably be better enabled to present itself as relevant in the modern world.

CHAPTER 7

BIBLICAL INTERPRETATION

All Christians agree that scripture holds a unique place in the shaping of Christian faith and practice. Interpretations of scripture, however, vary within different Anglican traditions. As the gap between the liberal and conservative wings becomes wider, with differing views about what is meant by biblical authority at the heart of their disagreements, Geoff described the role of the issue of homosexuality as *"the litmus test"* of one's orthodoxy.

This chapter examines the ways in which the Bible is used in the debate. Its focus is the way in which, while the Church stigmatises them on the basis that their lifestyle is contrary to biblical teaching, the gay interviewees employ alternative interpretations of the Bible to transcend the negative attitudes they encounter. The chapter shows that, rather than concentrate on possible interpretations of a handful of texts that appear to condemn homosexual practice, the gay interviewees emphasised biblical themes of God's love for all, principles of justice and Jesus' solidarity with the oppressed. It was to teach this Good News that they firmly believed the Bible should be exclusively used.

The texts that have traditionally been used to justify condemnation of homosexual practice are these:-

Genesis 19 tells the story of the destruction of Sodom. God was planning to destroy it anyway, because of all kinds of wickedness, not just sexual sin. When the angels arrived to let the people know, the men from the city surrounded the house where they were staying, proposing to rape them. Lot offered the men his virgin daughters instead!

Leviticus 18:22 and Leviticus 20:13 are probably the texts

most frequently quoted. They state that for a man to lie with another man as with a woman is an abomination, punishable by death.

In the New Testament, Paul writes in Romans 1:26-27 of God giving sinners over to shameful lusts for one another as punishment for idolatry. In 1 Corinthians 6:9 and 1 Timothy 1:10, the translation "homosexuals" is generally assumed for the original Greek words, although their meaning is ambiguous. Whoever these people were, they are included in a list of the unrighteous who will not inherit the kingdom of God in 1 Corinthians, and, in 1 Timothy, in a list of ungodly sinners for whom the law is laid down.

The Bible says homosexuality is wrong, or "A pretty sort of simple position"

The retired respondents, representing the traditional view still presented as the official position, believed that homosexual practice is wrong because the Bible says so. When homosexual activity was an offence, if Christians thought about it at all, the attitude of the majority would be that the tradition of the Church on all such matters had stretched unchanging across centuries and cultures. However, as Bishop Laurie Green writes, "Over the last few decades this secure stand of tradition has had the rug of accelerating history pulled from under it" (1990:119). This shift had caused most of the retired respondents to think about the issue of homosexuality more deeply than they had forty years ago, but nevertheless almost all still held the traditional biblical view. This can be equated to the approach of *Some Issues in Human Sexuality*, which studied every aspect of the matter yet still came to the traditional conclusion.

"*The* Church *is the interpreter of scripture and not the individual and in the last resort it is the teaching of the Church throughout the ages which really matters,*" was Richard's emphatic position. "*The Articles of the Church of England say about the Old Testament that the laws are not binding, except those that are moral. And that's a pretty sort of simple position,"* said Roy. Both these respondents believed St Paul's teaching was based on the Levitical laws on this matter and so also should be taken as binding.

The views of the respondents had not changed during the forty-year period, despite the rise in attention given to liberal interpretations. *"In the fifties, it was taken that the Bible was clearly against homosexuality. I actually still think that is the case,"* said Roy. Roger compared modern translations with the one he was familiar with, the Authorised Version, but felt that all translations are *"still quite affirmative on these texts."*

Liberal arguments were distrusted. Roy told me that he was *"not convinced by the arguments of a number of people, you know, Vasey of Durham and Boswell who wrote a book... The problem is that those who like me hold the conservative view go partly back to the ordinance of creation, male and female sort of thing."*

Given that these gentlemen came from a generation during much of which homosexuality was not tolerated by society, their entrenchment in their views is understandable. In a modern age, with much more known the phenomenon of homosexuality, as well as increasingly sophisticated biblical scholarship, which Bishop John Shelby Spong asserts "has simply not been made available to the man or woman in the pew" (1991:10), it is contended that similar entrenchment by the Church should be open to question.

Biblical condemnations, or "Singled out because it's sex"

When the gay interviewees were pressed on the subject of whether the Bible does actually say that homosexual practice is wrong, Gerald conceded, *"It is my interpretation, having looked into it, really very carefully as you might imagine, that the Bible is, on any frank reading of it, on the whole against same-sex activity. Gay sexuality should not be expressed physically, by any fair reading of St Paul. I think I would agree, insofar as you can match up historically with the situation we're in now."*

Does the fact that the Bible says it is wrong mean that it actually is wrong? *"There's a whole lot of other things in Leviticus as well. You know, this is something that's been singled out of a huge book on law,"* said Greg. Gus agreed: *"Three or four verses that people fasten on to, without all the other Jewish forbiddings. Thou shalt not this, that and the other. There are just these three or four things that people fasten on to, because it's sex."*

Looking further at the biblical condemnations, Greg mused, *"Jesus had nothing to say about it at all. There's nothing in the Gospels about it. The whole of the Sodom and Gomorrah story I think was more about hospitality. I mean, for goodness sake, there's Lot, and basically these angels appeared to destroy the city. The city wanted the angels, and the host says, 'No, but I'll give you my daughters.' I mean, hang on a minute! And St Paul, I think, was a misogynist anyway."* Grant had other thoughts about the Pauline verses. Quoting passages exhorting slaves to obey their masters and wives to obey their husbands as well as to keep quiet in church, he continued, *"It's interesting if you look at St Paul, because he was so conditioned by waiting for the Second Coming that he saw that there was no point in changing social conventions."*

Guy was disdainful of homosexuals who treat the biblical condemnations with any degree of seriousness: *"I hate the way gay people snivel. You know, 'Of course there are arguments in scripture against this.' You wouldn't expect a black person to say, 'Well, I know there are reasons why I might be a slave'!"*

Greg commented on the fact that the Bible also says other things are wrong, some of which are treated with less emphasis by the Church: *"When you look at the Ten Commandments, we seem to treat those almost dismissively. They're not part of the compulsory liturgy anymore, unless in a Prayer Book service. I mean, 'You shall not commit adultery' – The Church doesn't bat an eyelid these days about adultery. 'Thou shalt not steal' – Does the Church bother about that? 'Thou shalt not bear false witness' – Does the Church bother about that?*

Yet they've got this obsession about sexuality."

The views of the lay interviewees who were seeking ordination are also significant in considering the importance that should be placed on the condemnatory passages. Leo posed the questions, *"And at the widest level, there's the understanding of what scripture is anyway. I mean, is it a manual of theology and ethics? Or is it actually a living document?"* Lewis believed, *"I think what the Bible is asking is fidelity, and faithfulness and honesty. Not promiscuity and not indecency, rather than prescribing a particular manner."*

As Christians committed to the service of God, the gay interviewees clearly regarded the Bible as authoritative. Their view on *how* it is authoritative, however, had led them to different conclusions about what its contents mean for homosexuals from those of Church reports. They were adamant that, despite their profound respect for the Bible, they did not in any sense believe themselves to be disobeying its precepts in being in same-sex relationships.

Use of the Bible: "Picking and Choosing"

When considering the issue of biblical authority, Green asks an important question: "How do we know whether we have read into the text what we prefer to see there rather than what is in fact there?"(1990:120). The phrase "picking and choosing" was used by several of the retired respondents when speaking of how the Bible is and has been used.

Richard's opinion was that *"There has always been a tendency to interpret the Bible according to one's own stance, rather than to approach it objectively and to discern what it has to say."* Roland agreed that for a long time people have extracted the verses that suited them: *"I think the Bible has always been used in controversy in the way that it's being used now, with people taking particular verses and waving them and saying, you know, 'This settles the matter!'; instead of saying, 'There are elements in the Bible which have some bearing on this issue whatever it may be, homosexuality or stem cell research, and there are other principles and wider trends in the Bible which can be evoked perhaps on the other side'."*

The tendency to extract certain verses was considered to be prevalent in the current climate. *"It seems to me there is much more of an almost party examination of the Bible, when people have a particular case to put. You know, they're able to, as it were, pick and choose the bible, in a way that didn't seem to me so obvious when I was a theological student and working through parish ministry,"* said Ralph. Robert agreed that the majority of lay people do not read through the Bible as a continuum: *"I know a lot of people read the Bible daily. But they'll pick and choose which bit they want to read."*

This tendency was thought to be unfortunate. As Coulton asserts, "A responsible attitude to the Bible does not ignore some parts and highlight others" (2005:5). Roland's view was that *"If you're a Christian, you have to justify the things you do by your conscience. But to claim that it's all right to be whatever, whatever your predilection is, whatever your behaviour is, it's all right because it's in Psalm 114 verse 6 is absurd."* Robin stated, *"For me, the Bible is a gift to be used. But we worship God, not the Bible. The Bible is a book to be learnt from, not to hit people over the head with."*

Use of the Bible: "A Gospel of Hatred?"

The gay interviewees would agree strongly with the last statement, which resonates with the title of a book by Adrian Thatcher, *The Savage Text* (2008). As those most affected by the way the Bible is used to condemn their lifestyle, their views about the arguments employed were expressed with varying degrees of disdain. Their responses to questions about the role of the Bible in the debate yielded four ways in which it was thought to be used.

Firstly, it is used literally. When asked about Bible-based discussion, Graham replied, *"I haven't heard much Bible-based discussion. As I said earlier, I don't think it's any good arguing with evangelicals who think scripture is infallible. They're not going to change their mind."* Grant went further: *"One of the things which strikes me about some evangelical views of scripture, is that, to me, they treat scripture idolatrously."* This comment resonates with Thatcher's contention that in some parts of the Church, veneration of the Bible rivals or even exceeds veneration of God Himself.

Gareth thought the Bible is used pedantically. He had just read the typescript of a book in which the author was *"trying to be liberal from an evangelical perspective. He's saying, 'Look, if we translate the Greek and we look back to what the Hebrew might be for a particular term and the context of it, this is what we read.' And I just don't use scripture that way. It's a fantastically anal approach to text."*

There was much agreement with the retired respondents' indication that the Bible is used selectively. George thought that the condemnatory passages are *"often quoted out of context. I think, like all biblical passages, I think they've got to be used reflectively and responsively, with thought for the time and context in which they were written. And I think also, must be interpreted in the age in which we live."* *"I'm very uncomfortable about people just lifting passages out of scripture. Context is so important,"* said Grant.

"We are selective. Jesus wasn't married. Solomon and David had several wives and concubines, as did Abraham and Moses," Gareth stated. And Grant asserted that *"Everybody interprets scripture according to their own agenda, don't they. I mean, you start with what you think and then you look into scripture for its justification."* Michael Hampson accuses evangelicals of doing this, attributing to them the "insistence...that gay sex is somehow dirty, unhealthy and repulsive. This argument comes not from faith or scripture but from prejudice" (2006:156).

The idea that the Bible is used as a weapon to justify the rejection of homosexuals was mentioned by several of the gay respondents. Gareth's words on this subject sounded remarkably like Robin's quoted above: *"The Bible says a whole load of stuff and you can't just use it as a weapon to hit people with. The Bible's written so we learn about God's love for all of us because of who we are. And to use it as a thing to say, 'Well, God loves me, but doesn't love you', is not my understanding of what the good news of God is all about."* Gavin thought that, *"to use the Bible in that way is perfectly absurd actually. You might as well pick up any textbook off the shelf and start quoting from it. It seems to me to be pathetically immature. I think the Bible is far too important to use it in that way.*

Gordon said, *"I suppose, if the Church is to be called to account because of slavery, it will be called to account for this rejection as well. I mean, the Church has a long history of its failure to proclaim the Good News."* Canon Paul Oestreicher agreed when he wrote, "We have apologised to the former slaves; we have apologised to the Jews. We are, it seems, not yet ready to apologise to our lesbian and gay sisters and brothers" (Letters, Church Times August 7th 2009).

When speaking of the biblical arguments, Greg said ruefully, *"We talk about God being a God of love, and yet we're preaching hatred in a sense."* Thatcher contends that "The savage text makes hatred holy" (2008:5). What a sad indictment of the way the gospel message is presented to homosexuals. Yet the gay interviewees tolerate this distortion of what they believe to be the message of the Bible in order to be able to continue to serve the Church that perpetuates it.

Divine inspiration: its changing nature

2 Timothy 3:16 tells us that "All scripture is inspired by God." *Some Issues* explains that, for Anglicans, biblical texts in fact have "a dual nature. On the one hand, they are the 'word of God', texts inspired by God through His Spirit to be the medium of his self-communication to us. On the other hand, they are also human artefacts, created by specific human beings in specific human circumstances" (para 2.3.2).

While for some Christians, inspired means infallible, to be taken literally, many would agree with the World Council of Churches' assertion (1998) that "The Church is called to be a *hermeneutical community,* that is a community within which there is a commitment to explore and interpret anew the given texts, symbols and practices." It is quite possible to believe that the Bible is inspired by God without necessarily believing Him to be the ultimate author of every word. The distinction is explained thus by Spong: "Yes, for me the Bible is the means through which I hear, confront, and interact with the Word of God. No, the words of the Bible are not for me the Word of God" (1991:249). As Father Christopher Jamison, the Abbot of Worth Abbey, put it during the BBC programme, 'The Monastery' (2005), "The Word of God comes to me through the text."

In examining the nature of divine inspiration, the gay interviewees noted a number of the attributes of scripture. *"We have to accept that the Bible isn't one book. It's a series of books which were written in different communities at different times, culturally conditioned. The purpose of those documents was to give a sense of identity to the communities in which they grew up, and to give them some sort of pattern and model on which to live their life,"* said Giles. Furthermore, Gordon added, *"one has to conclude that the Bible knows very little about what we know about modern sexuality, psychology or human relationships. Neither does it know anything about modern science, but why should it?"*

Divine inspiration was therefore not perceived as something static in one age. *"I do believe scripture is inspired. But I also believe God continues to inspire through everything that has happened since. You know, through psychology, science, medicine, technology,"* said Grant. Giles agreed. He expressed concerns about reading the Bible too literally: *"I do believe [biblical texts] to be inspired, divinely inspired. But we have to be honest and say that if you go down the literalist line, of saying every single word is inspired by God, as many do, you do get in a bit of a mess then when you begin to approach the texts and see that there are things that don't add up, or contradictions. Like for instance, just an example, why does Luke say there were two angels at the tomb of Jesus and Matthew only has one? You could say, 'Well,* that's neither here nor there'. Actually it is here or there. If we're being literalist about this, let's be literalist about it, you know?"

"I think people are understanding now that the Bible isn't that sort of a book. You don't rush to it for a rule. You have to work out your rules for yourself. The Church helps you to work out a rule," said Graham. He went on to cite instances of issues on which the Church had reinterpreted its original understanding of scripture. Other gay interviewees also referred to such issues.

The issue mentioned most was that of slavery. "The Bible does not - wouldn't even have considered abolishing slavery. And yet that is rejected in modern life, even by fundamentalist evangelicals," Gordon pointed out. Graham agreed: "The Bible doesn't condemn slavery. It says you've got to be a good slave. It's very interesting in the discussion about slavery at the moment, nobody has said, 'Well, actually the Christian faith doesn't condemn slavery.' It doesn't. St Paul didn't think slavery was wrong. It was part of life. So the idea of development - I think people do realise that the faith develops; and you look at the texts and explain them." Guy's contribution was that he has "a friend who says he's longing to write a letter to the papers, saying something to the effect, 'Dear Sir, The Archbishop of Nigeria forcefully expresses his anxieties about western liberalism as expressed over homosexuals. While I might have some sympathy with his anxiety on this particular point, I can't help but feel that, were it not for western liberalism, he might find himself with manacles round his hands and I would buy him.' You know, you can't have it all."

Graham raised the question of the remarriage of divorcees: "Bible texts against remarrying are so strong. Much stronger than anything about gay relationships. And yet the Church has managed to say, 'Well, you can marry again, and it can be done in church'." Grant was also concerned about this: "The other thing about evangelicals is how they cope with divorce among their members. You could say that scripture is very anti-divorce. And yet they've come round on that, so if that's ok, why isn't homosexuality?" Gagnon asserts that divorce is a forgivable sin for those who repent, whereas the "serial, *unrepentant* character of much homosexual behavior [sic] sets it apart from the divorce issue" (Via & Gagnon 2003:47). If the definition of sin is separation from God as a result of breaking His law, the gay clergy, men of prayer, would emphatically deny experiencing such a separation on the grounds of the expression of their sexuality within committed relationships.

Another issue raised was usury: *"Lending money at interest is forbidden. I started a sermon once by saying that it is forbidden in scripture, forbidden by four general councils. Somehow or other the Church got round that one of course,"* said Graham. Of the Levitical laws, Grant pointed out that *"People are quite happy to wear mixed fibre clothes, aren't they?"* Gordon's contribution was sardonic: *"What I always say to biblical literalists is, 'I'll give up being a gay man when you stop eating shellfish and start stoning rebellious teenagers publicly in the market place'. Because it's all in the same book. And they say, 'Ah yes, but we know now that caning children and stoning rebellious teenagers in the market place is – we've learned from that'. Well, learn a bit more! That's all I just say to them: Learn a bit more!"*

The role of women is clearly very different in modern times from that expected in the Bible. Guy summed this up by saying, *"A few years ago at Matins, we had the reading, I think it's from Ephesians [5:22-33], all about husbands and wives and the relationships that should ensue. And we made, the vicar and I, our female colleague read it. And we sat there laughing. And she was cracking up while she was reading it. And that was great. That was a very good model of the interpretation of scripture. And the time will come when we read those passages [condemning homosexual practice] and do just the same thing. Because they come from a world* none *of us would want to go back to."*

Some Issues in Human Sexuality notes that biblical interpretation now takes place in many different contexts, and gives two possible answers to how Christians should respond to this. The first is that we must stick to the belief that biblical texts have specific meanings expressed by the words of their human authors but bear the inspiration and authority of God. The task of the interpreter is to discover the meanings and to discern their significance for today's world. The second is that the meaning of a text is relative to the people who interpret it. In the issue of the biblical passages about homosexuality, it is the meaning of the words that have come to denote this term that is crucial if conservative theologians are to be persuaded that the Bible does not contain outright condemnation of all homosexual practice.

Some Issues devotes a chapter to examining the work of different scholars on each of the passages traditionally taken as condemnatory, the main tenor of which is to determine what exactly it is that is being condemned. At the end of the rigorous examination, the chapter acknowledges that "there is room for a legitimate debate about the interpretation of the texts concerned" (para 4.5.1), but nevertheless refuses to deviate from the conclusion of the 1991 report. However, the gay clergy interviewed believed unequivocally that, not only was the understanding of the nature of sexuality entirely different at the time the passages were written, but the behaviour to which they refer bears no significant relation to the loving, committed same-sex relationships into which they themselves had entered in good faith. This firm conviction enabled them to respond to God's call to the ministry with clear consciences on the matter of their sexuality. Indeed, as the next chapter will show, they were in no doubt that their sexuality was part of their creation in the image of God.

CHAPTER 8

SEXUAL IDENTITY

It is important to remember that at the time when the allegedly condemnatory passages in the Bible were written, there was no word in either Hebrew or Greek for homosexual and, as far as we know, no understanding of the existence of homosexual orientation. This is why there has been so much debate about the meanings of the passages, which are by no means as clear as some writers would claim. In fact, the word "homosexual" was only coined in the late nineteenth century by German psychoanalysts, and introduced into English at the beginning of the twentieth century. Prior to this, the word "sodomite" was used to describe men who engaged in same-sex acts. However, this word did not indicate someone who did so because of a homosexual orientation since it was not understood that such a thing existed. Rather, sodomites engaged in such acts because of a perversion. This idea was prevalent until the nineteen thirties, after which psychologists such as Freud and Kinsey suggested various theories about the underlying causes of what was becoming recognised among a limited group as an orientation.

At the start of the period covered by this study then, the idea that homosexuality was not a perversion was still relatively new. It was in 1973 that the American Psychiatric Association concluded that there was no scientific evidence that homosexuality was a disorder, and removed it from its diagnostic glossary of mental disorders, with the International Classification of Diseases of the World Health Organisation following suit in 1992. Such developments, as well as evolving theories about genetic factors in sexual orientation, are thought by many to have a bearing on the morality of homosexual behaviour. Security in their certainty that their sexuality was part of the person created by God in His image played a significant part in the gay interviewees' ability to transcend the hypocrisy they encountered in the Church's approach to them.

Genetically determined so morally neutral, or "Like having dark hair or eyes"

When the gay interviewees were asked what they thought causes people to be homosexual, they gave similar answers. Guy replied, *"I don't think anybody* knows *what causes people to be gay."* Grant's view was, *"There are so many theories, aren't there, of causation, and nothing is ultimately the whole truth, is it."* And Gareth said, *"It's very interesting, that I think we've given up trying to find causes, actually, in psychoanalytic stuff. There are still people trying to look at that, but on the whole the debate has been, 'What do we now do? What do we do with people as they are?'"*

Thus it was felt that there is no concrete knowledge about causation, but that in society there is now more understanding of homosexuals than there was in the past. When Gerald studied what at the time were considered the *"new human sciences - psychology, sociology, psychiatry and so on,"* he decided that they had a *"different language, in terms of wholeness, healing and mental health"* from theology's. Graham felt that dislike of homosexuals was a cultural issue amongst the older generation: *"I remember my mother saying the most dreadful things about gay people. She's 97 now. She had no understanding of it. And of course, now there is more understanding."*

The gay interviewees were adamant that homosexuality is not a choice and cannot be cured. *"Nobody sets out to be homosexual. I don't see how anybody ever could,"* said Gus. Guy asked wryly, *"Why would fat middle-aged guys like me keep it going? Because actually our life would be far easier if we married. Think of the respectability, and the pleasure of having a home with children in it, and someone else doing the washing and the ironing and looking after you."*

Prior to the 2008 Lambeth Conference, the evangelical organisation Anglican Mainstream produced a book, *God, Gays and the Church* which included an American psychologist's theory of "reparative therapy" for homosexuals, and also testimonies from homosexuals who claim to have been cured. Graham had himself undergone *"analysis with a Jungian analyst. I even thought about going for LSD treatment, but I didn't. I chickened out. I was too scared. And twice a week I went to see this therapist. ...I honestly don't think it's possible to turn someone from homosexual to heterosexual. I did try, didn't I, for ten years, to change myself to be a heterosexual. It didn't work at all."* Greg had recently watched a programme *"where they were saying that some people are conditioned to homosexuality. I don't think they are. I mean, at the age of 12, when I think back, I just knew I was different. I knew I was attracted, not to men actually, but to other boys."*

Twenty years ago, Jeremy Marks started an evangelical organisation called Courage UK, which set out to change people who were tempted to adopt a homosexual lifestyle. Such a lifestyle was believed by Marks to be sinful and symptomatic of the moral collapse of society. However, in 2001, Courage UK completely changed its policy. In his book, *Exchanging the Truth of God for a Lie* (2008), Marks explains that, after years of implementing programmes to change subjects' orientation, he had come to believe that they were ineffective and that sexual orientation was much more innate than he had originally thought. He had also been shocked to find that some who had been disillusioned to find that they had not been changed as a result of his programmes had tried to commit suicide.

Theories that have been suggested in the past about the cause of homosexual orientation have included having a parental relationship that is in some way flawed. The gay interviewees did not give credence to such theories. Guy's view was, *"You can play all the games about dominant father, feeble mother, or feeble father, dominant mother, and then you can put people side by side, and your heterosexual friend has a dominant mother and a feeble father – So hang on a minute, why did it not work with that one? There is no theory that works satisfactorily in terms of nurture."* Graham pointed out that *"The old absent father idea would mean that all the people who were born in wartime would be gay, wouldn't they. And an over-possessive mother: all the Jewish race would be gay."* Grant felt that parenting theories would mean all siblings would have the same orientation: *"I grew up in a house where my brother was rampantly hetero-sexual... We had the same schooling and everything."*

The overwhelming opinion was, in common with the most recent studies, that sexual orientation is probably genetic. *"I'm not aware that there's anything in my background that made me homosexual. I was born a homosexual. I think people are born with their sexual orientation,"* said George. Gareth claimed that it is possible to recognise boys early on who are likely to be gay, *"and if you know their future you'll discover that they have become gay. So we are aware that there's something which seems to be very early, if not right at the start."* Greg agreed that *"It's genetic"*, as did Graham, who added, *"like having dark hair or eyes."*

Gerald's view was rather more complex: *"I think that it's, it probably is, predominantly, a genetic predisposition, but like all predispositions – and I'm thinking of many that have been identified in the field of mental health, such as schizophrenia and psychotic depression – it's the predisposition that's inherited, clearly. Experimentally, you can see that in families. But there's got to be a convergence of precipitating external circumstances for the predisposition to be triggered."* This resonates with the assertion made by Professor Michael King in an article in the Church Times (July 25th 2008) that "Genes are not the only factors involved, and environmental influences may be needed for genetic effects to be expressed." Professor King was the author of the Royal College of Psychiatrists' 'Submission to the Church of England's Listening Exercise on Human Sexuality' of 2007.

Gerald went on to contend that *"If it is genetically predetermined, then it is much more likely to be judged morally neutral."* Again this resonates with Professor King, who states in the same article, "All theological, philosophical, and moral debates about how lesbian and gay people should lead their lives and follow their religious beliefs need to take account of these premises" [that sexual orientation is a human characteristic formed early in life and is resistant to change]. The Church, however, does not consider them relevant in its conclusion that a homosexual lifestyle cannot be commended as the undistorted will of God.

The interviewees considered that Nature knows best in these matters. *"Some people would say that it's a very useful safeguard that 10% or whatever of people are homosexual, otherwise the population would explode,"* said Graham. Guy's view was *"If you were to tot up the value of the social contribution of gay men and women, I think you'd find a genetic reason why it's good that it's there."* George agreed: *"Some of our greatest leaders, Christian and otherwise, have been of homosexual orientation. Great heroes, people of enormous courage, in the military and in every walk of life. I think homosexuality has a significant contribution to make to our society, and indeed to the Church."*

The Royal College of Psychiatrists' report, mentioned above, makes it clear that, in their sexual behaviour, homosexuals have the same responsibilities as heterosexuals. The interviewees agreed. Gerald felt that active homosexuality is defensible *"as long as it doesn't result in behaviour that is harmful either to the individuals concerned or to others."* Some interviewees felt that marrying would be harmful behaviour. *"If a gay person got married, that would be regarded as sinful. It would be abusive of the partner, and it would potentially create chaos for the family,"* was Guy's view.

"It's how we live with that homosexuality that's important," said George. This is a vital point in considering the suitability of homosexuals for the priesthood. A promiscuous homosexual would not be commended by this study, any more than a promiscuous heterosexual would be. The interviewees were attempting,

without the support that the Church gives to their heterosexual counterparts to enter lasting partnerships, to make the best use of what they believed to be their God-given sexuality.

Changing views, or "Maturity and grace"

In considering how acceptable they felt homosexual relationships to be, the retired respondents talked of many of the same issues as those mentioned above. *"What causes people to engage in homosexual relationships is the be all and end all of it,"* said Ralph.

Ronald expressed the view that was prevalent in his youth. Like many of his generation, he was still convinced that *"a lot of homosexuality is perversion"*. Roger, too, thought that *"It is unnatural. It is a disorder in sexual behaviour."* Unlike the House of Bishops, they had not studied later psychological studies, so it is understandable that they still expressed views prevalent in their youth.

Robert's approach showed more empathy with the gay interviewees' own experience: *"One of the conservative evangelical approaches is that 'of course we can put these people through a training course and make them into a happily married man' or whatever. Well, rubbish. I've had youth clubs where twelve-year-olds were quite noticeably different in their relationships to what you might call your average twelve-year-old."*

Roger was probably summing up a common position amongst heterosexuals in the Church when he explained that he found it difficult to understand how strongly homosexuals feel in their attraction to the same sex because *"of course sexual feelings with men for me were not to be thought of. It was girls."* Roy recognised that *"to [homosexuals] a relationship with a woman would be just as distasteful as a relationship with a man would be to me."*

Some of the retired respondents reported that they felt differently now about the acceptability of same-sex relationships from their views of forty years ago. This was in part due to the fact that society's views have altered. Roy said, *"The thing that has changed is that at the time when conservative views were held in the fifties and so on, it was assumed that homosexuality was some kind of perversion. It was assumed that a great many of them ought to be marrying a woman, but out of their own bloodymindedness, you know... What* has *become recognised, I think, is that it does now appear to me to be clear that some people are born this way." "I think I, and perhaps a lot of other people, have come to understand the situation a lot better,"* said Robin.

Ralph had not only come to understand the situation better, but also explained his changed approach: *"There are probably a lot of things that I'd have said no to 40 years ago that maturity and, you know, grace have given a bit... and, well, maturity encompasses a great number of things, doesn't it. It encompasses a whole change in society and science and the arts and all sorts of pressures that come to you from all different directions. Maturity isn't just about ageing is it."*

Reservations were still held, however. Some of these were affected by the different ways in which homosexuals display their sexuality, resonating with the views of the gay interviewees that the morality of homosexuality is inextricably linked with the way it is exercised. *"Homosexual people vary as much as anyone else. There are some who are a liability to themselves and everyone else. There are others who quietly get on with it,"* said Robin, implying that the latters' relationships were more acceptable to him than the formers'. Robert had had a homosexual curate: *"Fantastic parish priest, the best curate I ever had. Much admired and much loved by men and women."* On the other hand, Robert did not like *"stage queers. You know they've got 'Oh ducky' and all the sort of mannerisms that have nothing at all to do with the sexual inclination of anybody."* Roland agreed that he found some aspects particularly difficult: *"I find some of this flamboyant same sex propaganda quite offensive. Distasteful."*

Popular stereotypical presuppositions, or "I'm not dressed in a pink leotard"

The gay interviewees believed that much of the negative feeling that homosexuality generates is caused by mistaken assumptions and false stereotypes. Duncan Dormor explains that the natural desire of humans to feel secure about the boundaries of their groups and the moral values that bind them together leads collective anxieties to be placed on 'outsiders', who are then seen negatively, such as asylum-seekers or people who are religiously or racially different. "All of these are symbolic constructions; that is, they are identities, groups of people hated primarily as imagined invisible abstractions with stereotypical characteristics, rather than in the more concrete form of Patrick or Errol or Maria who lives next door and may not in fact be recognized as a member of the labelled group"(Dormor & Morris 2007:80). Jeffrey John agrees that "Knowing an ordinary gay couple is the best antidote to prejudice and the best way of destroying the ludicrous stereotypes and suspicions that still lurk in the mind of many. People soon come to realize the lifestyle doesn't differ much from their own" (2000:54).

Six different stereotypical presuppositions were suggested by the gay interviewees. Firstly, gays are not manly. Gerald remembered his parents' horror on learning that a friend's son was going to be a ballet dancer: "*I immediately blushed. You know, I knew the gay connotation of that at once. And one of my sisters said, 'But Daddy, I do ballet. What's wrong with that?' And so my father saying to me, 'Well, we understand, don't we?' And then said something about manliness or manhood or something. I was sitting there in confused silence.*" Graham agreed that being homosexual "*hit against manliness. If you were gay, you were not manly. And I think it was the effeminate end of the gay world that was visible. I mean, I'm not against Larry Grayson, but I think they did us a great disservice in many ways. And Mr Humphries. It's all very well to have a good laugh. But people thought that all gay men were like that.*" Julian Clary was mentioned by Grant as an effeminate stereotype who has influenced people's perception of what homosexuals are like.

The second misconception is that gays are paedophiles. *"There are still people out there who believe that homosexual men prey on children and on vulnerable adults and that sort of thing, which is not the case,"* said George. Grant had been angered by someone asking whether it was appropriate for a gay member of his congregation to run the Sunday School: *"I said, 'In my experience, it is people who are at terms with their sexuality who are the least danger to children. It's people who aren't. Those who abuse children tend to be supposedly happily married people.'"*

That gays break up marriages was another presupposition. Guy suggested that what people know of homosexuals in this respect is what he called a pastiche: *"The married man in his forties or fifties, who just can't cope anymore. Either he's caught cottaging or there's an ill thought out relationship with someone older or younger or whatever. One way or another, the family breaks up, he leaves home, she daren't come to church anymore because she's so ashamed, the children are appalled, they never come back to church for years and years if at all, and there you are. That's homosexuality breaking up a family."*

Yet another assumption is that gays will make a pass at you. Gordon recalled a friend of his who was *"tiny, and bless him, a pansy in the old-fashioned way. And I remember a big rugby player at college who was frightened to death of him. I think he really thought that something could happen, and he was frightened of that. And that has much more to do about the insecurities of sexuality."*

Other ways in which gays are thought to be different were mentioned. Guy thought that in fact negative feelings are caused by a *"visceral reaction to difference. I think it's just the same as, 'I don't have any colour prejudice. But I don't want my daughter bringing one home!'"* Grant felt that ignorance also plays a part. He had visited some parishioners recently, *"and they were talking about how terrible, how disgusting it is, all these gay people. 'They all ought to be put on a desert island and allowed to die out'. And I said to* them, 'Have you ever thought that it actually takes two heterosexual people? Where do you think gay people come from? Mars?'"

The final presupposition mentioned by the gay interviewees was summed up in the fact that, ironically, they had been told by parishioners that they did not know any homosexuals. Vasey states that "Gay people tend to be invisible to straight people. It means that many straight people's image of gay people is created by the media and the more extravagant manifestations of the gay movement rather than by gay friends" (1995:168). Gordon had found this to be the case: "They always talk about 'these people', don't they. It's never about you."

Grant had attended deanery meetings where things he found insulting had been said about homosexuals: "And part of me wants to say, 'Look, here I am. I'm not dressed in a pink leotard. I'm just here, dressed very conservatively. This is me. This is my life you're talking about. You talk about 'them out there', when there are some of us sitting in this room. This affects every fibre of our lives."

Our sexuality, or "What I believe is just me"

When the gay interviewees spoke about their sexuality, several common themes emerged. Although Philip Giddings of Anglican Mainstream stated on the Channel 4 documentary, 'Gay Vicars' (2006), that he did not "accept the categorisation 'Be Gay'", all the interviewees said that they had known they were homosexual from an early age. For example, Gus explained, "I've known I've been homosexual ever since I was a child. It's been the mainspring of my life." And Giles said, "I think probably I've always known that I was gay. I think I've never been aware of any attraction other than to people of my own gender."

Gerald's realisation that he was homosexual was "in the context of understanding very clearly that it was absolutely disapproved of, and thought to be sinful, which did trouble me, as a child." For Gavin, the same understanding led to positive feelings: "I think there was quite a bit of me that liked to feel that I was different – that I was special, *actually. On a certain level it worried me, of course, and I think I probably was aware, and this might be a bit of hindsight talking, that life would be a bit tricky. But nevertheless I enjoyed the sense that I was special. But at the same time I also knew that I would never share that with anyone; that it was my secret. I knew that it was something that I could not share, because everybody else thought it was wicked."*

Despite recognising as children that they were attracted to other males, for some interviewees they did not understand the full implications of this until later. *"I assumed that it would go away,"* said Gerald. Gordon had thought *"that everybody felt the same as me, but that they got married and had children... And I thought how wonderful it would be to be a dad... I didn't have the kind of feelings that I now realise people have, but it didn't strike me that that was odd. Because I'd never heard the word."*

Two interviewees tried to be cured. Graham's attempts have already been mentioned. Grant *"went to the student-counselling centre, with a view to see if I could get some sort of cure for my feelings. I had about one session and I realised that wasn't possible."* Despite knowing themselves to be homosexual, several of the interviewees had girlfriends when they were young. Gus said, *"Of course, everybody wanted me to get married, and so I went out with some very pretty girls. But I never could get any excitement from them. And so that had to be honestly faced. And of course I knew I was excited by beautiful men."* However, none of the relationships seem to have been sexual. Gordon recalled, *"I had a very nice girlfriend in the sixth form and it was, I can see now, largely platonic – almost entirely platonic really. But we were huge friends and, you know, gooey eyed and in love and all that kind of stuff."*

Only Graham had gone further than this and had actually got married. He found the recollection painful: *"I really kidded myself that I could probably get married. So on my last day as a curate, a woman arrived on the doorstep who I'd been very fond of at university. And it just seemed as if God was saying, 'Look, here she is.' We went out together, and I just thought that things would work themselves out.*

So I said, 'How about getting married?' Of course it didn't last. The marriage was annulled after a year. It was a terrible time, I can tell you. It's easy for me just to sort of mention it now, but it was the most dreadful time… Obviously we didn't have children because we didn't have sex."

The lack of shame about their sexuality was unanimous amongst the gay interviewees. Giles said that, if he should be asked if he were gay, he would not deny it: "Because that would be in fact to deny a fundamental part of my humanity, and if we are made and created in the 'imago dei', then that's actually an insult to God to deny an essential part of who and what you are." Gordon declared, "I'm damn well not going to be ashamed of what I believe is just me." It was felt, however, that the Church encourages homosexuals to be ashamed. "It's not something I'm ashamed of," said Grant, "but somehow the Church puts us in this position whereby we feel this sense of shame." Gus spoke vehemently: "I think it is evil that people say God is against me. Because it's making me a non-person."

Despite the Church's position, lying was not considered to be an option. "I'm certainly not prepared to lie about it," said Giles. Guy stated, "I don't believe in walking into a room and saying, 'Hi, I'm gay!' But, with very few exceptions, when people have asked, I've always told them. And I've never had a bad reaction."

"On a day-to-day basis, it is something that I hardly think about," said George, encapsulating the final theme of this dimension, that the gay interviewees just get on with life. Giles explained, "My sexuality obviously is an important part of who and what I am, but it doesn't determine everything else. And in that sense, one tries to integrate that aspect of one's life into one's whole personality and work. I think that with sexuality, as with other aspects of ones life, if one area becomes too dominant or important, then you risk getting sort of unbalanced in some way." He, like most of the others, tried to be discreet: "I've never been a member of campaigning groups or gone on marches, or said 'Look at me, I'm a gay priest'," he pronounced. "I'm hugely discreet about my orientation. I hope I'm not a person who's overtly *camp or effeminate,"* said George.

"All our friends know that we're gay, and they welcome us on holiday as well as to their homes, in the same way in which they're welcome here. Most of them are heterosexual couples. So that we try to live a very normal, happy life," said Giles. He added, *"To me there have always been much more important things. It's just part of who and what you are. It isn't very different from saying, you know, 'I play the piano', or "I like roast beef" or whatever it is!"*

"You don't choose it," said Gus, *"but when you are, you make the most of it. Because when you find you are, you just get on with it."* This is what the gay interviewees are doing: "just getting on with it", despite the negativity of the Church, living their lives in the service of God within the context of a sexuality that they did not choose.

The importance of how homosexuality is exercised: "Permanent, faithful, stable"

The title of Jeffrey John's book, *Permanent, Faithful, Stable,* describes the kind of homosexual relationship that he defends as not incompatible with scripture. He makes it clear in all his writing that this is the only kind of homosexual practice that he does defend, and indeed it is the only kind that this book defends. "Of course there is no such thing as the perfect Christian gay relationship, any more than one can point to the perfect Christian marriage", he writes. Nonetheless, his knowledge of "many relationships based on this kind of Christian understanding and commitment has proved to me that it is not naïve or impracticable" (2000:5).

This is the ideal to which the gay interviewees aspire, and which they have achieved with varying degrees of success. Two have always been single. *"I have no partner, have not had a partner, do not seek a partner, have never sought a partner,"* maintained George, who felt it important for homosexuals to be celibate. *"I've never had a partner, because I think the Church made it very difficult to have a partner. But I had people I loved, you know,"* said Gus.

The other interviewees had been part of relationships that were faithful and stable, with varying degrees of permanence. Some had had several committed partnerships. As a young man, Gerald had had various relationships which lasted *"two or three years. When I was thirty I decided I wanted to live with someone I met."* He had been with his current partner for a number of years and they had had a civil partnership. Grant was with his first partner for 4½ years, but, when he moved to another parish, *"I did rather a silly thing. I felt I was in this staid relationship and I wanted to see the bright lights, so I finished with B, which was one of the silliest things I've ever done in my life really."* He had since had another long-term relationship, which had recently ended.

At the time of their interviews, several of the gay clergymen were in long-standing stable partnerships, which, in keeping with the wide age range of those interviewed, varied in length from 5 years to 38 years. When Giles met his partner, *"we both felt instinctively that this was going to be a relationship that was going somewhere. We felt an instant affinity with each other. Now five years on, we still feel that as keenly as ever and we genuinely believe that we are life partners. It might not happen – who knows? But that's what we believe and the way in which we approach the relationship. So it is a deeply committed, monogamous relationship."* Greg said, *"How I exercise that [his sexuality] is more important than anything else, and D has certainly been the stabilising influence on that. The last seven years in August we've been together. There's been no question on either side of straying. It's been a very solid relationship."*

Gavin always felt he was *"the marrying type... I met J, and we've been together twenty years."* Gareth had been with his partner for 24 years, while Graham and his partner had *"been together 38 years this year. And fortunately, he wasn't the reason why I separated from my wife, otherwise I'd be feeling immensely guilty. He came along afterwards, and we've been together ever since."*

These stable relationships, some of which have lasted as long or longer than many heterosexual marriages, are nevertheless forbidden by the Church of England. In 1991, *Issues in Human Sexuality* did contain glimmers of hope for the future. Despite forbidding clergy to live in such partnerships, the Statement concedes that it is important to recognise the common ground in the emotional experiences of heterosexual and homosexual couples. Both, it recognises, speak of the attraction called 'falling in love', the longing for an exclusively close relationship with the beloved, the wish to share one's life with them and the desire to express affection sexually. When such relationships are genuinely unselfish and loving, growing "steadily in fidelity and in mutual caring, understanding and support", such as those described by the interviewees, the partnerships that are formed, homosexual as well as heterosexual, are described by the report as "a blessing to the world around them"(para 4.6).

Although it concluded that "Heterosexuality and homosexuality are not equally congruous with the observed order of creation" (para 5.2), and that therefore clergy, as people who "not only preach but live the Gospel" (para 5.13) must be banned from entering same-sex partnerships, the report's attitude to lay homosexuals was much more positive. It declared that, although the bishops were "unable...to commend" homosexual partnerships among lay people, they would show respect for "free conscientious judgment" and would not "reject those who sincerely believe it is God's call to them" (para 5.6). These extracts indicate a considerable degree of sympathy for homosexuals by the bishops at that time, and one might well have expected that, given the decisive moves towards tolerance in society, the Church would by now have taken the short step from its 1991 Statement to demonstrate similar respect for the "free conscientious judgment" of its homosexual clergy.

Through their writings and some recent public statements, as well as through things said privately to the interviewees, an indeterminate but considerable number of bishops, as well as Rowan Williams, have indicated that as individuals they would support such a step. That the House of Bishops as a body has not felt able to do so, despite the changed understanding of the phenomenon of homosexuality, is due in no small part to the increasingly powerful evangelical wing of the Church of England and the Anglican Communion. For groups such as those represented by the prominent organisation Anglican Mainstream, homosexual practice continues to be condemned as unscriptural and homosexual orientation considered to be capable of cure. The House of Bishops has therefore felt it necessary, whatever the beliefs of its individual members, to maintain its traditional stance for the sake of unity.

The gay interviewees, however, were enabled to transcend the Church's stigmatisation of their sexuality by their firm conviction of its being an integral part of the person God made in His image. As such, they saw no reason to be ashamed of it, to hide it, or to try to suppress or change it, though, as with all characteristics, they felt it important to exercise it within the context of Christian values, in this case love and faithfulness. They were in no doubt that they were loved and valued by God as gay representatives of His diverse creation.

CHAPTER 9

THE TRANSCENDENT VOCATION

Why they stay, or "Called by God"

Earlier chapters of this book provided evidence that the policy of the Church of England towards homosexuals constitutes an injustice characterised by hypocrisy. Analysis of the interviews with both the retired respondents and the gay clergymen showed that for decades an unofficial policy of "don't ask, don't tell" has been employed when ordaining homosexuals, when placing them in parishes, and when dealing with them pastorally. The report that is the nearest thing the Church has to an official policy, *Issues in Human Sexuality,* actually states that it is not appropriate for bishops to seek out and expose clergy whom they may suspect to be in a sexually active same-sex relationship. As Gordon suggested, bishops are pleased to be able to use this paragraph as an excuse not to ask questions that would both cause them embarrassment and require them to take disciplinary action. Evidence has been given that at least one bishop publicly assents to the conclusions of *Issues,* whilst privately writing to offer good wishes to a clergyman entering a civil partnership. Moreover, several interviewees recounted how bishops had been guests of them and their partners and yet had publicly denounced homosexuality as incompatible with scripture. Even Rowan Williams, the Archbishop of Canterbury, supports the conclusions of *Issues* and the ban on practising homosexuals being consecrated as bishops, despite publishing work questioning the traditional teaching of the Church on this issue before his appointment to the post.

A significant reason for this apparent hypocrisy is anxiety on the part of the House of Bishops not to antagonise the evangelical wing of the Church, who not only condemn homosexual practice increasingly strongly as being incompatible with scripture, but also wield a lot of power. In the Church of England, this power is financial. Earlier chapters showed how the forced withdrawal of Jeffery John as Bishop-designate of Reading was largely caused by the threat of evangelical parishes to withhold their parish share.

While at the beginning of the period covered by this study, a homosexual with a partner had to be equally discreet in society and in the Church, it is now the case that in any secular job there is no longer any need for discretion. Indeed, in any other walk of life, discrimination against homosexuals is illegal. That the Church, which follows the fully inclusive teaching of Jesus, should be the one organisation legally allowed to operate discrimination is another example of hypocrisy.

The questions addressed in this chapter are therefore: Why do homosexual clergymen tolerate the way they are treated by the Church? Why do they not all leave it and thereby enable themselves to live openly with their partners without fear of exposure or discrimination in seeking preferment?

From the analysis of the interviews with the gay clergymen, four themes emerged that explained why these men are prepared to tolerate it. None regretted being ordained and none had considered leaving the Church. What follows will not only make their reasons for this clear, but will also demonstrate their commitment to the institution that stigmatises them.

Firstly, the interviewees accepted that no organisation is perfect. As everyone will have experienced, whatever profession one is in, there will always be aspects of it which cause one annoyance. Gavin pointed out that *"We do not live in a perfect world, which is in every way convenient for each of us as individuals. We all have to make choices about how much we are prepared to compromise."* Just as the world is not perfect, the Church cannot be either. *"We're not a perfect organisation. No church will ever be. I think that's why we are Christians, because we recognise our short-*

comings and our failings and want God to build up our lives," said Greg.

Gareth recognised that, despite the official negativity and the fact that "as an institution, it's struggling, as institutions do," within the Church there are areas where homosexuals can find acceptance and much going on to help them determine how to live Christian lives. Gavin explained that, as part of a diverse organisation, he was "happy, for the most part, to rub along with other clergy with whom I may profoundly disagree about this issue among others."

Secondly, the interviewees respected the House of Bishops, both as a body and as individuals. They expressed understanding for the reasons behind bishops' wish to turn a blind eye to homosexuals, and sympathy for their position of having to preserve unity. It was generally agreed that it was unnecessary to cause trouble by giving the bishop any personal information for which he had not asked. Collusion with the "don't ask, don't tell" policy was seen as the sensible way forward. "I have a good respect for the bishop. I like him. He's always been very kind to me. And I don't want to compromise that relationship. I see no point. I don't want to make him feel he's got to say something unpleasant to me," said Gavin.

"I think it must be a terrible job being a bishop, terrible job. Because they get got at by lots of people. The last thing they need is that. They're struggling to keep the whole show afloat," said Gareth. Because of his sympathy for his bishop's position, he had "not wanted to create a problem for him at all. He's just following, I presume, the line of the Church." Graham agreed: "I've always worked on the understanding that I don't tell them. Because you put them in a very difficult position."

There was particular sympathy for the Archbishop of Canterbury's position. The interviewees understood his overriding desire to preserve unity, both within the Church of England and within the Anglican Communion, and so, despite their disappointment that he had not fulfilled their hopes by remaining true to his liberal views, most accepted the reasons behind this. Grant summed up feelings expressed by several interviewees about the Archbishop: *"I feel very sorry for Archbishop Rowan. Because he's now the sort of hitting boy for everybody, isn't he. A lot of people were his supporters before he was a bishop, when he was in the Jubilee Group and writing a paper for LGCM. And now he seems to have drawn back on that. He's not good enough for the conservatives and he's seen as a traitor to the liberals. I think it must be a terrible position to be in. And Jeffrey John had been an old friend of his too."* Gareth added another factor in the Archbishop's position, the negative attention of the media: *"If Rowan says anything which is at all controversial, the press are out for him. I feel for him."*

It should be apparent from these expressions of empathy, and indeed from the extracts from the gay interviewees' contributions throughout this study, that these are men who possess qualities and principles that are, their sexuality aside, in keeping with their positions as clergymen. The third theme that emerged, "It's not about Me", emphasises further their selfless commitment to the organisation that condemns their lifestyle.

This theme underlay much of the gay clergymen's response to probing about the reasons they continued working within the Church, regardless of their feelings about its approach to homosexuals. Their overriding priority was to serve God and their congregations. Concerns about the Church's negativity were of secondary importance.

With the exception of Guy, all the interviewees were adamant that campaigning was not appropriate. They would agree with Oliver O'Donovan, who writes that the possibility of the debate moving forward "from the present stalemate" depends to a large extent on "how the Christian gay movement addresses the Church. So long as it is content to present itself in the guise of injured protest, armed with a list of rights it has been denied, then, whatever does happen, a meeting of minds will not happen" (2003:36).

"*I am not a campaigner. I never have been, but I am happy to have the conversation if the matter is raised,*" said Gavin. Grant agreed: "*I'm not a gay activist. I think I would see myself as wanting to be just accepted as a gay man in an ordinary community. I have great problems with niche churches, like the Metropolitan Community Church,* [run and congregated by homosexuals,] *because I think the Church ought to be representative of the whole of humanity, with its diversity.*"

The reasoning behind the view of most of the gay interviewees that it was inappropriate to draw ostentatious attention to concerns about their own stigmatised position through any kind of militancy or political activity was that this would be likely to compromise the mission of the Church. Geoff was adamant that "*No clergyman would want to publicly take part in a discussion that is going to have a negative effect on the mission of the church unless he is a rebel rouser.*"

It was generally agreed that the mission of a clergyman was not about himself. "*Clergy should just quietly get on with their jobs and not worry about presenting themselves. It's about presenting Christ within that community,*" said Gareth. Raising one's personal life and concerns was unlikely to be helpful in presenting Christ. "*My 'stuff' is normally totally irrelevant in my encounters and it is rarely appropriate in this strictly professional context to 'disclose' and that obviously includes my sexuality and my relationship. I have no problem about people knowing that I am gay; it is quite simply that to talk about myself in this way in this context would be inappropriate,*" explained Gavin.

The function of a clergyman is, then, simply to get on with the job of helping the Church to help other people within the environment in which he is employed, and not to hinder the furtherance of this task by standing against the Church on this issue. When faced with criticism of a sermon about AIDS, Gordon did not enter a dispute; he just "*pursued my policy of just keep on keeping on, quietly and politely*" until the criticism died down. Geoff felt that the increased profile of the debate about homosexuality was hampering gay clergymen in their attempts to perform their responsibilities: *"Polarisation has been distinctly unhelpful for those of us who are trying to get all sorts of different people to work together harmoniously... The public debate has created a difficult position for clergy who are simply wishing to function within the institution and to fulfil their role within it."*

The majority of the interviewees were protective of the Church's reputation and mission, and were clear that they did not want to be the cause of any harm being done to these. When he had been asked directly by a Baptist minister whether he was in a homosexual relationship, Greg gave an ambiguous answer because, if he had replied in the affirmative, it would have had a negative effect on many people, and not least on the build up of links between the Baptist and the Anglican community. He summed up feelings expressed by several interviewees when he asserted, *"I don't want to see the Church getting bashed any more than it has been."*

When they had been faced with prejudice, interviewees showed Christian charity in their understanding of the people concerned. *"You learn about people, that they are misguided. They just don't understand, so I don't get terribly upset. These people said some very unkind things, but I've been used to being in situations where I shut up as a priest and I've learnt not to take it personally. It's ok. That's them. That's their generation,"* said Grant. Gordon felt no animosity towards the parishioner who had criticised him to the Bishop for preaching about AIDS, but said of her, *"She can't be blamed for coming from the background she comes from, the time that she comes from, and having the experiences she's had. And, whereas I didn't intend to stamp on feet, some feet are more delicate than others."*

The overriding theme of this dimension, however, was the conviction of all the gay interviewees that they had been "Called by God" to the work of an ordained priest. There could therefore be no serious thought of leaving the Church however unhappy they were with its approach to them. The chapter now moves forward to explore this concept of the "Transcendent Vocation".

Vocation as a homosexual, or "God calling me with my sexuality"

Becoming a priest is unique in relation to other occupations in that it is not enough simply to want to be a priest or think one would be a good one. It is necessary to convince those with responsibility for selecting those to undergo training and ordination that one has received a call from God. As Kenneth Mason writes, possessing appropriate virtues and abilities are not enough to make someone a priest, "only the grace of a specific vocation can do that"(2002:108). The procedures by which selection is accomplished are rigorous. A potential candidate has to be seen by several different people before even being recommended, or not, to go before a selection board. A vital question to which all are endeavouring to discern the answer is whether the candidate has indeed received a call, or vocation, from God. John Pritchard lists the nine criteria that candidates for ministry in the Church of England have to fulfil. The first is "Vocation. Candidates need to be able to speak realistically about their personal journey of faith and how they came to feel they may be called to ordained ministry" (2007:3).

Since the gay clergymen had been ordained, they must necessarily have convinced a number of prayerful and experienced people that they had such a call. Although it is unlikely that any of them alluded to their sexuality during the selection process, in their interviews for this study all indicated in one way or another their strong belief that God had called them, not despite their homosexuality, but with it.

Some traced their vocation back as far as their childhood. Giles said, "I was aware of a vocation to the priesthood almost as early as I can remember... My mother says that when I was a small boy, when people said to me, 'What are you going to do?', I used to say, 'I'm *going to be a vicar'."* Gerald described himself as a *"cradle clergyman"*, as he always assumed this was what he would do. George remembered that when he was fifteen, he went to his incumbent and told him he wanted to be a priest, and the incumbent replied that he wasn't surprised: *"I think I felt quite a distinct calling to be of service as a priest."*

Greg thought that others had recognised his vocation before he did: *"Not that I felt called to the priesthood, but there was a sermon that the vicar was preaching about vocation and about God's calling, not necessarily to the priesthood. And he said, 'There's always somebody in every congregation who is being called by God'. I felt everybody looking at me."* Gordon's view of his vocation was that *"you find or perceive a calling through doing"*. He had helped in churches from a young age and realised that *"the church was in desperate need of priests. And I remember thinking, you know initially, seeing the problem and not really particularly thinking I would have anything to do with it, until after a while, over a period of time, it became obvious really."*

Two interviewees, however, could pinpoint their calling to a particular moment. Guy did not become a Christian until the end of his schooldays and was confirmed as an undergraduate: *"I knew at the time that I had to come back. I have a memory of the feeling which later on I worked out was 'I have to go back. Confirmation is not going to be enough for me.' The thing about vocation is you can't help it. It gets you."* For Leo, the call came even later: *"Within two or three months of turning forty, I had this very specific experience of sense of vocation. Just like a sentence coming into my head saying, 'You should be a priest' or 'I should be a priest'. I can never remember which it was. But anyway, 'should be a priest' was the essence of it."*

Several of the gay respondents further emphasised their certainty about God's call. Giles expressed his desire to be happy with his partner when they moved in together, but that he felt it imperative to continue in his calling as a priest. Gus was convinced that, when his spiritual director suggested that he should enter the chaplaincy that was to form his main ministry, *"God was saying that. Yes, I'm sure I was given this commission by God."*

Greg had left theological college after a year and had not intended to go back: *"I thought that was the end. But God had other ideas."* He felt himself led to return and subsequently to be ordained. Gordon *"said to the Bishop when I was interviewed, 'You and I might think it is rather stupid that God calls people like me, but I do think that He did.'"*

For some, the calling from God was actually entwined with the realisation of their homosexuality. Grant spoke of how he realised that he was gay while he was at secondary school, *"though at first I thought it was a phase I was passing through. And I realised I had a vocation to the priesthood even more strongly then. So the two went hand in hand."* For Guy, the Christian gospel of redemption for people on the fringe encouraged him as he was realising that he was gay: *"So for me, the two things are always inextricably bound together. I mean you can't get involved in the business of love without God, and you can't get involved in the business of God without love."* Gavin explained, *"What perhaps happened in terms of my realising that I wanted to be ordained, and also my developing understanding of my sexuality, was that I had a sense that the one would compensate for the other. And that my being ordained would make me acceptable."*

Given the Church's disapproval of homosexuality, it had been necessary to think carefully about whether ordination was possible or appropriate. *"Obviously I did have a struggle at about the age of eighteen, whether or not it was compatible to be of a homosexual orientation and at the same time to seek ordination to the priesthood,"* said George. But any doubts were overcome. Guy told me that while he was *"humming and hawing"*, Jeffrey John encouraged him to go forward. Gordon *"knew that potentially it could all go horribly wrong. But I always thought that it wouldn't go horribly wrong if I simply got on with the job."* And for Gavin, *"It was a joy, not a problem. Because what happened was that I found my safe place in the Church. I found my home in the Church. I found my friends in the Church. I found my family in the Church. And I still think of my Church as my family."*

Lewis was seeking ordination at the time of his interview. He had realised his sexuality at a young age, and his perception of this in relation to his vocation was, *"If you feel something's right with the whole pit of your heart, then you've just got to pursue it. I think you'll get yourself into more trouble if you try and deny one of those things."*

So the conviction of the gay respondents that they had received a call from God can be seen, experienced as a "transcendent voice that defines and justifies the self as it guides and empowers the work of ministry" (Christopherson 1994:222). Their vocation had indeed helped each of them to justify his "self" in that they saw in it an affirmation by God that, in choosing them to minister as priests, He accepted them exactly as they were, together with their sexuality. This knowledge not only guided and empowered them as they undertook ministry already recognised as a source of stress (see Fletcher 1990), but also to endure the additional stress and difficulties caused by the Church's negative position. The way in which the call was "transcendent" is discussed in the next and final dimension, as the chapter moves forward to demonstrate specifically how their vocation led the gay respondents to a determination to remain within the Church, regardless of its official approach to them.

The Transcendent Vocation, or "For better or worse"

Keenan (2009) suggests that the reason there is a gap in discussion about how gay clergy who do not feel able to be open about their sexuality (which, given the Church's negative position, is most of them) manage their identities is that such clergy in some way 'lose' the gay aspect and become 'clergy'. The interview contributions of the respondents to the present study entirely support this suggestion. For the gay interviewees, the overriding theme of the contributions that explained how they managed to transcend the hypocrisy of the Church was that they had been "Called by God". It was this sense of vocation to serve God as a priest that took precedence over concerns about issues to do with their sexuality. As shown earlier, they felt it inappropriate to take any kind of stand against the stigmatisation to which they are subject since this would be likely to interfere with their mission as a priest. They were prepared to tolerate the Church's negativity as an unfortunately necessary part of living out their vocation.

Because of this Transcendent Vocation, there could be no serious thought of leaving. *"I've felt called to the priesthood for as long as I can remember, ever since I was a little boy,"* said Grant, adding, *"I couldn't imagine not being [a priest]."* Gordon declared, *"For better or for worse I'm going to go along with [my calling], until such day when the Church says 'Go away, we don't want you any more'."*

The respondents had been subject to various forms of hypocrisy during the forty-year period covered by this study, but none more so than Giles, who, when summoned to discuss possible preferment, was told that, although his sexuality presented no problem as long as he was discreet about it, no preferment was open to him if he proposed to be open about his relationship with his partner. This hypocrisy surely might have been expected to prompt him to leave the Church. However, on the contrary, he declared, *"I wanted to continue being a priest. Which was the thing I believed in. I've believed in it since I was a boy and I still believe in it passionately with my heart. Within my heart, that is what God has called – is calling me – to do."*

Thus the certainty of God's call to them enabled the gay respondents to transcend everything to which they were subjected by the Church. However great the negativity they encountered, they were determined to be faithful to their vocation. There was no doubt in their minds that this was God's will for them, regardless of the Church's insistence, stated in *Issues in Human Sexuality*, that physically expressed same-sex relationships are not acceptable for clergy.

Gerald stated that his reasons for pursuing his vocation, *"even though I had a clear understanding of the church's formal position, were actually related to my refusal to accept the position of a victim in regard to my sexuality. My family had served in the ordained ministry of the Church of England over some generations and since the Church had itself validated my vocation, I was not going to be put off by what I regarded as its historically understandable but erroneous views on homosexuality."*

The number of gay clergymen whose voices have been heard in this study is small. Nevertheless, from the data they have given it is possible to gain insights into the experiences and attitudes of homosexual clergymen in general. It is the contention of this book that clergymen in same-sex relationships are not the "abomination" that evangelicals would claim on the basis of Levitical law. They are principled men, with a strong sense of vocation, anxious only to do God's work of building up His Kingdom. They are doing so against a background of prejudice on the part of sections of the Church and of hypocrisy on the part of the House of Bishops. Yet, despite the fact that, as has been shown, it is more difficult to live as a homosexual clergyman today than ever before, the majority continue to do so.

Why do they tolerate the situation? This chapter has summed up the feelings of the gay interviewees in the form of four themes. Firstly, in accepting that no organisation is perfect, despite private disappointment with the Church's approach, they are prepared to put up with it. Secondly, notwithstanding the hurt caused by the double standards they perceive as being contained in the pronouncements and methods of the House of Bishops as a body, their respect for individual bishops and for Rowan Williams enables them to rise above this. Thirdly, their overriding concern is not to present themselves and their personal agendas, but to preach the Gospel. And fourthly, they believe passionately that they have been called to the priesthood by God and, as such, they have no option but to tolerate the inadequacies of the context in which they feel certain God has placed them. Their sense of vocation is stronger then the sense of stigma under which they are compelled to work. This "Transcendent Vocation" was the most significant finding of my research project.

The discernment of whether someone has truly been called by God as he or she claims is no easy matter. That the clergymen represented are prepared to tolerate all the difficulties and injustices presented in the preceding pages in order to live out their vocation must be evidence worthy of careful consideration that they have indeed been called by God to minister as priests. It would be good to think that such consideration might be given by those whose theology and approach to biblical interpretation may previously have led them to perceive that such a calling to a practising homosexual is not possible. At the very least, it is hoped that it will be conceded that the individuals quoted in this study are honourable men who exemplify the selfless dedication to the service of God required by the Church of its clergy.

So, what are the implications for the Church of the findings of this study? They lie in an invitation to look again at its approach to its homosexuals in the light of the Transcendent Vocation. Is the behaviour condemned in Leviticus and Romans really the same issue as the loving, faithful partnerships into which the interviewees have entered? Does the fact that they have entered partnerships of the kind that their heterosexual counterparts take for granted really make them unsuitable to serve God by ministering to their congregations and preaching the Gospel? Is their strong sense of vocation to be taken seriously, or is it in each individual's imagination? If the latter, how did the Church come to verify it and recommend their training for ordination?

Conservative evangelicals may well continue to conclude that the relationships into which these men have entered are contrary to scripture, that they are unfit to be clergymen and that they must have inveigled their way into ministry by lying about their sense of vocation. The theology of such readers will probably also lead them to feel that partnered gay people in general should not be made welcome in churches unless they can be persuaded to repent and seek reparative therapy.

If this is the collective feeling of the majority of the members of the House of Bishops, then of course the conclusions of their statements and reports must stand. However, it has been clear from recent utterances by some bishops as well as from evidence given in this book that this is not a generally held view. It is hoped that, by presenting the lived experiences of gay clergymen in this way, the House of Bishops might be prompted to consider afresh the justice of its rulings. More than twenty years after its publication, the present position is still that outlined in the 1991 report, *Issues in Human Sexuality*. Although partnered lay people would probably not find a welcome in evangelical churches, the report offers acceptance to lay people who enter gay partnerships in the sincere belief that it is God's call to them, but refuses to accept the same sincere belief in gay clergy. After reading the stories of gay clergy, does this still seem just or defensible?

As has already been suggested, the Church of England's official approach is steered by its vociferously evangelical wing, as well as by vociferously evangelical members of the Anglican Communion. It is hoped that the House of Bishops might collectively consider afresh whether this agenda really reflects the Gospel that the Church wishes to preach. Is the most important message of the Gospel to prescribe what people are doing consensually within loving relationships, or is it to preach God's love? Is it in keeping with the Gospel to stigmatise and exclude people on the basis of a handful of biblical texts? How do such actions reflect God's love?

It is my hope that the lived experiences of the gay clergy

whose stories and deeply held beliefs and values are presented here will make an important contribution to the listening process, enabling the House of Bishops to consider the above questions in the light of the Transcendent Vocation. It would be good to think that a start might be made to rectifying a situation which not only is unjust and unsatisfactory, but compromises the mission of the Church within a society that has come to accept homosexuals unequivocally. I hope that the presentation of these lived experiences might play some part in prompting the hierarchy to consider whether it is desirable for the future of the Church of England to follow the agenda of vociferous evangelicals or whether it should be possible for bishops and archbishops to stand up for the equality of homosexuals without fear of evangelical reprisals.

It would be naïve to suggest that changes of policy on this issue would not invite serious repercussions. A positive step would seem to be that parishes might be encouraged, on the basis of scripture, to show the same Christian charity as the homosexual interviewees in a preparedness to live with diversity. The ferocity of the debate since 2003 has principally concerned the consecration of gay men as bishops. It would seem sensible first to come to some practical official decision about homosexuals being ordained in the first place. Could both sides not be encouraged to come to the same mind as they originally did over the ordination of women? Would a pragmatic first step not be to agree that some churches could elect to accept a gay priest while others could elect not to do so? Discussion about the consecration of homosexuals as bishops could be entered once it was officially possible to be a gay clergyman living openly with a partner. The findings of this study offer fresh consideration of whether it is possible for such a clergyman to be honourable, principled and called by God.

REFERENCES

Bailey, D.S. 1952. The problem of sexual inversion, in *Theology*, LV, 47-52

Bates, Stephen. 2005. *A Church at War.* 2nd edition; London: Hodder and Stoughton

Buchanan, Colin. 2006. *Taking the Long View.* London: Church House Publishing

Christopherson, R.W. 1994. Calling and Career in Christian Ministry. *Review of Religious Research*, 35:3, 219-237

Church House Publishing. 1987. *General Synod Report of Proceedings, vol.18, no. 3.* London: Church House Publishing

Clergy Consultation. no date. [Online]. Available at: http://www.clergyconsultation.co.uk/index.htm [accessed: 21/04/09]

Coleman, Peter. 1989. *Gay Christians. A Moral Dilemma.* London: SCM Press

Coulton, Nicholas. (ed.) 2005. *The Bible, The Church and Homosexuality.* London: Darton, Longman & Todd

Cretney, Stephen. 2006. *Same-Sex Relationships: From Odious Crime to Gay Marriage (Clarendon Law Lectures).* Oxford: OUP

Crockett, A. and Voas, D. 2003. A Divergence of Views: Attitude change and the religious crisis over homosexuality. *Sociological Research Online.* [Online]. Available at: http://www.socresonline.org.uk/8/4/crockett.html [accessed: 17/02/09]

Dormor, Duncan and Morris, Jeremy. (eds.) 2007. *An Acceptable Sacrifice? Homosexuality and the Church.* London: SPCK

Fletcher, B. C. 1990. *Clergy under Stress: A study of homosexual and heterosexual clergy.* London: Mowbray

General Synod Board for Social Responsibility.1979. *Homosexual Relationships – A Contribution to Discussion.* London: Cio Publishing. ["The Gloucester Report"]

Green, Laurie. 1990. *Let's Do Theology.* London: Mowbray

Hampson, Michael. 2006. *Last Rites: The End of the Church of England*. London: Granta Books

Heskins, Jeffrey. 2005. *Face to Face: Gay and Lesbian Clergy on Holiness and Life Together,* London: SCM Press

House of Bishops. 1991. *Issues in Human Sexuality*. London: Church House Publishing

House of Bishops. 2003. *Some Issues in Human Sexuality*. London: Church House Publishing

House of Bishops. 2005. Civil Partnerships – A pastoral statement from the House of Bishops of the Church of England – 25th July 2005. [Online]. Available at:

http:// www.cofe.anglican.org/news/pr5605.html [accessed: 12/01/09]

John, Jeffrey. 2000. *Permanent, Faithful, Stable.* 2nd edition; London: Darton, Longman & Todd

John, Jeffrey. 2003. Christian Same-Sex Partnerships, in *The Way Forward? Christian Voices on Homosexuality and the Church,* edited by T. Bradshaw. 2nd edition; London: SCM Press, 44-59

Keenan, M. 2008. Freedom in chains: Religion as enabler and constraint in the lives of gay male Anglican clergy, in *Religion and the Individual,* edited by A. Day. Aldershot: Ashgate, 169-182

Keenan, M. 2009. The gift (?) that dare not speak its name: Exploring the influence of sexuality on the professional performances of gay male Anglican clergy, in *Contemporary Christianity and LGBT Sexualities,* edited by S.J.Hunt. Aldershot: Ashgate, 23-37

King, Michael. 2008.How much is known about the origins of homosexuality?, Church Times July 25th

Lambeth Conference 1978. Resolution 10. [Online]. Available at http://www.lambethconference.org/resolutions/1978/1978-10.cfm [accessed 8/9/12]

Lambeth Conference 1988. Resolution 64. [Online]. Available at http://www.lambethconference.org/resolutions/1988/1988-

64.cfm [accessed 8/9/12]

Lambeth Conference 1998. Resolution I.10. [Online]. Available at http://www.lambethconference.org/resolutions/1998/1998-1-10.cfm [accessed 8/9/12]

Marks, Jeremy. 2008. *Exchanging the Truth of God for a Lie: One man's spiritual journey to find the truth about homosexual and same-sex partnerships.* Chichester: Courage UK

Mason, Kenneth. 2002. *Priesthood and Society.* 2nd edition; Norwich: Canterbury Press

McCord Adams, Marilyn. 2005. Sexuality without taboos, in *The Bible, The Church and Homosexuality,* edited by N.Coulton. London: Darton, Longman & Todd, 36-48.

Nolland, L., Sugden, C. and Finch, S. (eds.) 2008. *God, Gays and the Church: Human sexuality and experience in Christian thinking.* London: The Latimer Trust

O'Donovan, Oliver. 2003. Homosexuality in the Church: Can there be a fruitful theological debate? in *The Way Forward? Christian Voices on Homosexuality and the Church,* edited by T. Bradshaw. 2nd Edition; London: SCM Press, 2-36

Peart-Binns, J. S. 2007. *A Heart in my Head: A Biography of Richard Harries.* London: Continuum

Pittenger, Norman. 1970. *Time for Consent: A Christian's Approach to Homosexuality.* London: SCM Press

Pritchard, J. 2007. *The Life and Work of a Priest.* London: SPCK

Robinson, J.A.T. 1963. *Honest to God.* London: SCM Press

Spong, John Shelby. 1991. *Rescuing the Bible from Fundamentalism.* San Francisco: HarperSanFrancisco

Thatcher, Adrian. 2008. *The Savage Text: The Use and Abuse of the Bible.* Chichester: John Wiley and Sons

Tomlinson, J.W.B. 2004. The Anglican Tradition of Controversial Bishops. *Modern Believing,* 45:3, 31-38

Tutu, D. 2007. Foreword, in *An Acceptable Sacrifice? Homosexuality and the Church* edited by D. Dormor and J. Morris. London: SPCK, ix

Vasey, M. 1995. *Strangers and Friends.* London: Hodder and Stoughton

Via, D. O. and Gagnon, R.A.J. 2003. *Homosexuality and the Bible: Two Views.* Minneapolis: Fortress Press

Williams, H.A. 1982. *Some Day I'll Find You.* London: Mitchell Beazley

Williams, Rowan. 2002. *The Body's Grace.* 2nd Edition; London: Lesbian & Gay Christian Movement

Williams, Rowan. 2003. Knowing Myself in Christ, in *The Way Forward? Christian Voices on Homosexuality and the Church,* edited by T. Bradshaw. 2nd Edition; London: SCM Press, 12-19

World Council of Churches. 1998. *A Treasure in Earthen Vessels.* [Online]. Available at: www.wcc-coe.org/wcc/what/faith/treasure.html [accessed: 14/10/05]

Yip, A.K.T. 1999. The politics of counter-rejection: Gay Christians and the Church. *Journal of Homosexuality,* 37 (2), 47-63

CHRISTIAN
ALTERNATIVE

Throughout the two thousand years of Christian tradition there
have been, and still are, groups and individuals that exist in the
margins and upon the edge of faith. But in Christianity's
contrapuntal history it has often been these outcasts and
pioneers that have forged contemporary orthodoxy out of
former radicalism as belief evolves to engage with and
encompass the ever-changing social and scientific realities. Real
faith lies not in the comfortable certainties of the Orthodox, but
somewhere in a half-glimpsed hinterland on the dirt track to
Emmaus, where the Death of God meets the Resurrection, where
the supernatural Christ meets the historical Jesus, and where the
revolution liberates both the oppressed and the oppressors.

Welcome to Christian Alternative... a space at the edge where
the light shines through.